Santa Clara County Free Library

California

Alum Rock

Campbell

Cupertino

Gilroy

Los Altos { Main
            Woodland

Milpitas

Morgan Hill

Saratoga

Reference Center-Cupertino

For Bookmobile Service, request schedule

Sunset
Washington
TRAVEL GUIDE

By the Editors of Sunset Books
and Sunset Magazine

Lane Publishing Co. • Menlo Park, California

Research and Text:
Bob Thompson
Maureen Williams Zimmerman

Coordinating Editor: Linda J. Selden

Design: Cynthia Hanson

Cover: Snow-crowned Cascade peaks tower over rafters on the Skykomish River. Most Washington river trips last for one day; the many dams prevent longer runs. Frequently the outfitters encourage rowing and paddling by the passengers. The cold waters of Washington's rivers are best run when they're highest, in spring and early summer. A few trips are scheduled in the fall. Photograph by Cliff Hollenbeck.

Acknowledgments
Many thanks to the following individuals for their special help in putting together this book: Kathy Balcom, M.J. Haney, Bonnie Henderson, Judith Leraas, Jay Moynahan, Nance Reznicek, Priscilla Sabin, Chrys Tindell, Lori Vanderbilt, Julie Williams and Dan Youra.

And additional thanks are due to many people at many departments, agencies, bureaus and chambers, who responded generously to our requests for information.

Photographers
TOM ALGIRE: 3. GLENN CHRISTIANSEN: back cover. ED COOPER: 6 top, 46 bottom, 54, 107, 115 bottom, 123. KEITH GUNNAR: 35 top, 46 top, 62 top, 74, 82, 87, 90 bottom, 95 top, 118 top. CLIFF HOLLENBECK: 14, 38 top. L.J. LINKHART: 30 bottom, 102, 118 bottom. CINDY MCINTYRE: 19 top. DON NORMARK: 38 bottom. HARALD SUND: 6 bottom, 19 bottom, 22, 35 bottom, 43, 51, 59, 66, 90 top, 99, 110, 126. HAROLYN THOMPSON: 30 top. BOB WATERMAN: 95 bottom, 115 top. DOUG WILSON: 27, 62 bottom, 79. ART WOLFE: 71.

Cartography
Roberta Edwards, Tim Kifune, Ells Marugg, Jack Doonan, and Rik Olson.

Sunset Books
 Editor: David E. Clark
 Managing Editor: Elizabeth L. Hogan

First printing May 1987

Table of Contents

7 Introducing the Evergreen State

10 The City of Seattle

32 Puget Sound

44 The Olympic Peninsula

60 Southwest Corner

72 The Cascade Mountains

96 Columbia River Gorge

104 Central Washington

116 The Eastern Edge

127 Index

SPECIAL FEATURES

9 Statewide Information Sources

13 Salmon . . .
King of Washington's Sport Fish

20 Washington's Clams

29 Wineries and Microbreweries

36 Puget Sound Ferry Routes

68 Indian History in Washington

80 Hints for High Country Hikers

89 Paul Bunyan Games

92 Freshwater Fishing

113 The Cowboy at His Best

In the lush greenery of an Olympic Peninsula rain forest, Soleduck Falls courses down a gentle slope. Hikers can cross the wooden footbridge to follow one of the many hiking trails in the region.

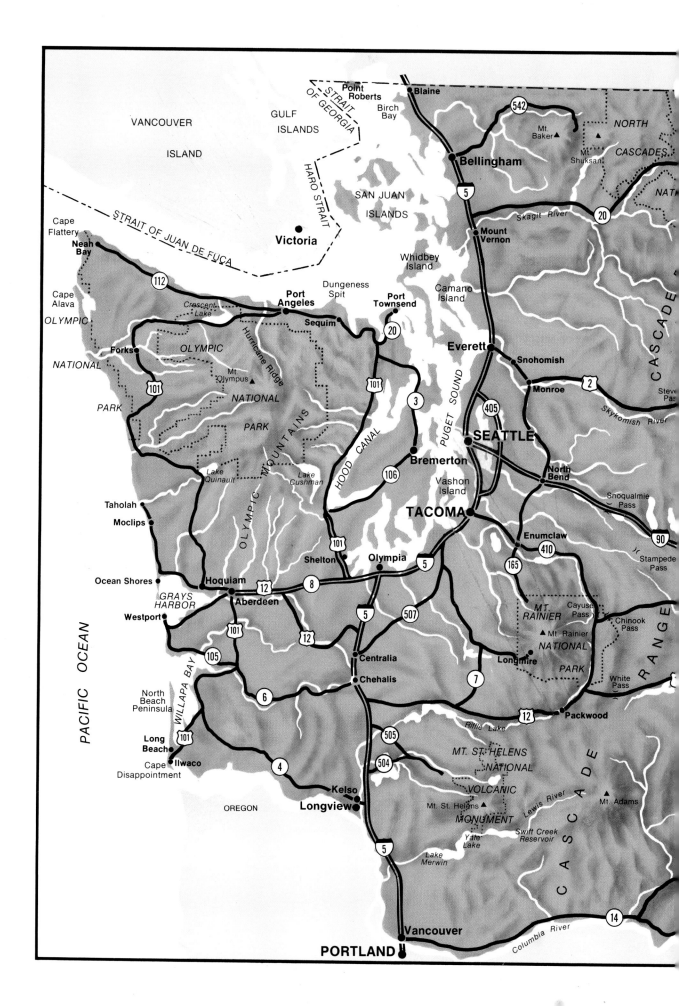

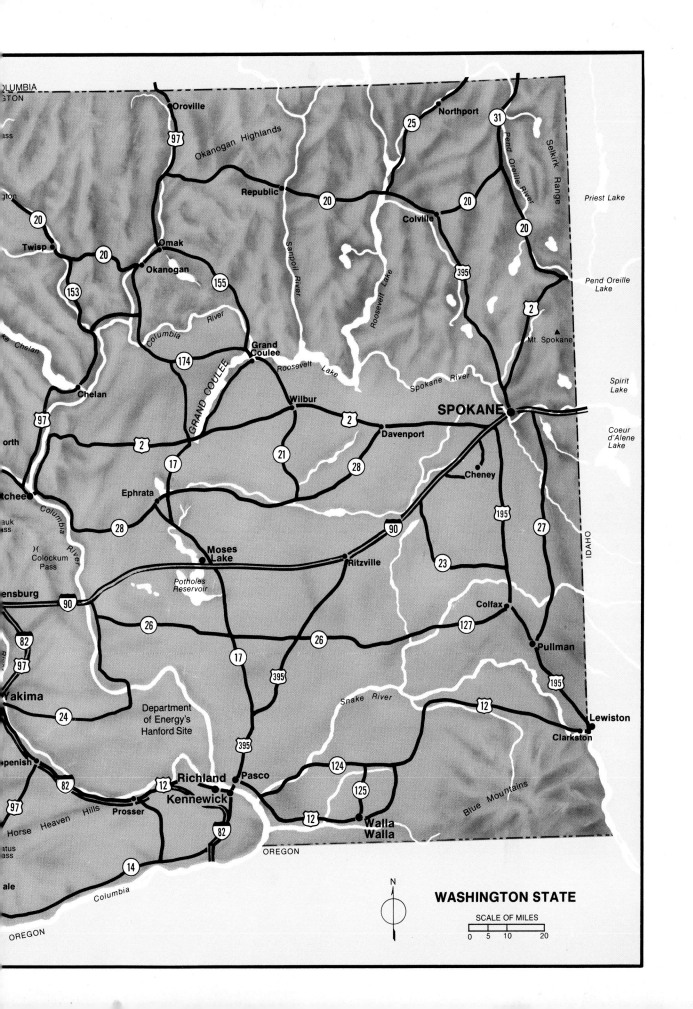

WASHINGTON STATE

SCALE OF MILES
0   5   10   20

N

Two states in one

In the cool, wet western half of Washington (below), a far-ranging ferry system is a vital part of the highway network where Puget Sound cannot be bridged. In warm, dry eastern Washington (right), wheels can go almost anywhere one cares to drive them. Nothing symbolizes better the sharp divisions caused by the towering Cascade Mountain range. For residents and visitors alike, the split yields an astonishing diversity of recreational pursuits.

Introducing the Evergreen State

Every now and again some literal-minded geographer tries to tell the world that Washington is designed all wrong—that the state should be divided somewhere just east of the Cascade Mountains. The western half should be joined with western Oregon into one coastal state, while the eastern half should include eastern Oregon and probably Idaho, too.

Unofficially, some things work out along these lines. Portland serves as the metropolitan center for much of southwest Washington, while Spokane plays a major urban role for many eastern Oregonians, as well as for residents of Idaho.

The literal-minded geographers draw their conclusion upon the spine of the Cascade Mountains. The mountains form a high, nearly unbroken barrier to passage between east and west in Washington. More important, they break the flow of sea air from the Pacific toward the interior so sharply that the west side has true climax rain forest, the east side true desert.

Because of the Cascades, little Washington—330 miles north-south by 460 miles east-west—has more diversity of terrain and climate than entire nations on smoother parts of the earth's crust.

Because of this, no sensible redefinition of state boundaries is likely. The natives, happy with two states for the price of one, would revolt.

Where to Go? What to Do?

Washington is to a tremendous degree an outdoor state: a mecca for hikers, skiers, hunters, campers, anglers, boaters, divers, bicyclists, even golfers and tennis players.

The range of choice for every outdoors sport is bewilderingly broad because of varied terrain and climate. And choice is made harder by proximity in a small area. Imagine how different the boating is on open ocean waters, sheltered Puget Sound, on the Columbia River, or any of scores of lowland lakes. Fishing is just as varied. Even the seasons open unexpected realms of choice. Snow skiers can compete on the Fourth of July, sailboaters in January.

The city of Seattle stands out for the urbanity only a major population center can offer. Yet while home to a highly praised opera company, major universities, and national football, baseball, and basketball teams, Seattle, like the rest of the state's cities, is still a comfortable place for an outdoors person. In Seattle, local business people can commute from suburbs to work—or to University of Washington football games—aboard boats. Profitable salmon fishing takes place within direct sight of downtown office windows and long bicycling trails depart from well within the city limits.

Throughout the state, smaller communities have worked to create their own special character—often achieving new sophistication against a backdrop of historical interest.

This book divides Washington into eight readily identifiable regions with names familiar to residents of the state: Seattle, Puget Sound, the Olympic Peninsula, the Southwest Corner, the Cascade Mountains, the Columbia River Gorge, Central Washington, and Spokane and the Eastern Edge. The Washington State Tourism Development Division uses eight similar, though not identical, denotations in its publications.

Each of the state's regions shares some characteristics with others but remains sharply distinct. Predictably, the basic differences stem from terrain and climate.

The Puget Sound basin outside Seattle, from Olympia north to the Canadian border, is the most populous region of the state. Nonetheless, it guards an outdoorsy character. Fishing—mostly salt, but with ample freshwater opportunities—is, along with boating, a major attraction.

The Olympic Peninsula, between Puget Sound and the ocean, takes a long step further in the direction of unspoiled wilderness. In a way, it is a microcosm of the whole state. A high range of mountains in the middle parallels the Cascades, leaving a shoreline ranging from rocky open ocean to placid sheltered arms in Puget Sound. The steep-sided mountains create a true rain forest on the west, in the process wringing out so much moisture that a small plain just to the east must be irrigated.

Southwest Washington in many ways bridges the small gap between the Puget Sound basin and the Olympic Peninsula. Not only is it neighbor to both, but its qualities fall between those of the other regions. Its Pacific shoreline is gentler and more accessible than that of the peninsula. Its interior, on the other hand, is a shade more rugged and less populous than the Puget Sound country. Its prime outdoor attractions are ocean fishing for salmon, razor clamming, every kind of freshwater fishing, and hunting.

The Cascades are the special province of hikers and campers in summer, skiers in winter. Parklands in this lofty, seldom-broken range are well developed for both purposes. Curiously, Mt. Rainier National Park has some of the gentlest, most accessible hiking and camping of any part of the range, which generally grows more rugged from south to north. The true seeker of wilderness solitude goes straight to North Cascades National Park. For skiers, every mountain pass has opportunity.

The Columbia River Gorge is, in everyday terms, a practical corridor for commerce, the easiest all-year route between the coast and the interior. More important, it is a special place—an awesome gap carved through immovable mountains by the irresistible force of the Columbia River at its fullest. There is some fine fishing to be done in the river and in the mountains rising above it, but just looking around can be reward enough.

Central Washington—the great basin of the Columbia—holds most of the state's cowboys and Indians. In more recent times, since Grand Coulee and other dams brought irrigation water to the parched hillsides, it has become home also to agriculturalists of every stripe, but especially apple growers, vineyardists, and wheat ranchers. In this sprawling region are most of the state's dude ranches, wilderness packers, and other horse-borne enterprises. Rivers and lakes provide some of the most reliable freshwater fishing in the state. Hunters favor the region, in some places for deer, in others for upland game birds.

Eastern Washington is known for its rolling wheatlands, especially the Palouse country between Spokane and Walla Walla. Its farmers work their land dry instead of with irrigation. North of Spokane, rugged pine-clad mountains focus recreation in a few places—primarily around lakes and ski slopes.

As easy as the state is to see in geographic blocks, it is even easier to consider activity by activity. The following quick summary is meant to guide readers with particular interests to more detailed information within the book.

Golf. Golf has been a popular recreation in every corner of Washington for decades. Nowhere are courses entirely absent; in few places are they even scarce. In green and growing western Washington, most mature courses are tightly treed. The emphasis is on accuracy rather than distance (which is hard for high handicappers to get on rain-softened fairways). In eastern Washington, courses tend to be more open and not so much longer.

Some of the toughest tests for golfers are at Port Ludlow, Sequim, and Leavenworth. Kayak Point (north of Everett) and Meadow Springs in Richland are considered among the best all-around courses in the state. Spokane's municipal system has two outstanding courses. Public courses are noted throughout the book, usually within the description of towns.

Tennis. Seattle and environs offer the greatest number of public play courts and clubs. Most of the towns along interstate freeways have good courts, many of them lighted to extend the short northwest season.

Bicycling. Bicyclists may shudder to think of mountainous Washington as a place to ride. In fact, the state is full of cycling enthusiasts who have developed a substantial number of trails in varied terrain. Seattle and its suburbs (especially those east of Lake Washington) have a host of marked trails, many in relatively open countryside. Also, the town of Redmond is a center for both road and velodrome racing.

Away from the urban environment, favored cycling areas include the hilly San Juan Islands and the flat northeast corner of the Olympic Peninsula.

Hiking. Three national parks, seven national forests, many wilderness areas, over a hundred state parks, and numerous county and local parks hold at least 2,000 miles of marked trails, ranging from the Pacific Crest Trail down to the popular seashore hike in Olympic National Park.

Because of their extent and their huge parklands, the Cascades hold the best-known and most-used areas. However, they are far from alone. The whole Olympic Peninsula is crisscrossed with trails. Less known is the Wenaha Tucannon Wilderness in the Blue Mountains, in the extreme southeast of the state.

Newcomers to the northwest and/or to wilderness hiking might profit from reading the cautionary notes on page 80.

Camping. Most of the same parks and regions that make hiking a major recreation in Washington state allow camping of some sort, from roadside with recreational vehicle to deep wilderness tent camping.

In summer, pressure on the more accessible parks can be intense. The national parks, national forests, and state parks have established a single information source, the Outdoor Recreation Information Office (address and phone number below). From Memorial Day through Labor Day, the state parks operate a toll-free information line, 1-800-562-0990. Some of the state parks take reservations for campsites, but camping throughout the state is basically first come, first served. Campsite reservation forms are available from the Information Office or the individual state park; allow fourteen days for processing.

Skiing. Every Cascade pass has one or more ski resorts; among the major ones are four near Snoqualmie Pass (I-90), Crystal Mountain (State 410, near Mt. Rainier), White Pass (U.S. 12), Stevens Pass (U.S. 2), and Mission Ridge (off U.S. 2 near Wenatchee). Mt. Baker is east of Bellingham at the end of U.S. 542. Two areas, 49° North and Mount Spokane, are close to Spokane; Bluewood is in the southeast corner. Limited-operation skiing is available near Waterville, Chelan, Port Angeles, Leavenworth, Omak, Tonasket, and Wenatchee.

Cross-country skiing is developing throughout the state. The Methow Valley has been the leader, but Leavenworth and Ski Acres (I-90/Snoqualmie Pass) also have set tracks.

Fishing. Few states offer a more varied fishery than does Washington. Salmon is the main game for many, especially at Westport and Ilwaco, but also all around Puget Sound. Winter steelheading is another major sport. The Olympic Peninsula and the Puget Sound region are the prime spots, although in rivers rather than in salt water. The Columbia River from its mouth all the way up to the British Columbia border, is a major freshwater fishery. Trout and kokanee are planted in every lake and stream that does not support its own native fish population.

Washington's fishing seasons, tackle restrictions, bag limits, and regulations are among the most complicated in the country. Contact the state's Department of Fisheries and Department of Game (addresses listed below) for detailed information.

Boating. Puget Sound, from one end to the other, is the great boating capital of Washington. Rental craft are available at marinas along both shores. The other great waterway is the Columbia, with its tributary the Snake. Using these two rivers, a boater can put in at the Columbia mouth and not leave the water until the craft reaches Lewiston, Idaho. The area around the Tri-Cities (page 100) is a sunny hub for Columbia and Snake boating. In addition to these waterways, there are hundreds of lakes ranging from 55-mile-long Chelan down to modest ponds; boat launches and rental agencies on these make a long enough list to fill a telephone book for, say, Tacoma.

Statewide Information Sources

Department of Natural Resources,
Public Lands Bldg., Olympia, WA 98504.
1-800-562-6010.

Outdoor Recreation Information Office
(National Parks, U.S. Forest Service, Washington State Parks), 1018 First Avenue, Seattle,
WA 98104. (206) 442-0170.

Pacific Northwest Ski Areas Association, 1326
Fifth Ave., Seattle, WA 98101. (206) 623-3777.

Washington State Department of Fisheries,
115 General Administration Building, AX-11,
Olympia, WA 98504. (206) 753-6600.

Washington State Department of Game, 600
North Capital Way, GJ-11, Olympia, WA 98504.
Olympia: (206) 753-5700; Seattle: (206) 775-1311.

Washington State Dept. of Transportation,
Public Affairs Office, Transportation Building,
KF-01, Olympia, WA 98504. (206) 753-2150.

Washington State Office of Archaeology and
Historic Preservation, 111 West 21st Avenue,
KL-11, Olympia, WA 98504. (206) 753-5010.

Washington State Tourism Division, General
Administration Bldg., Olympia, WA 98504.
1-800-562-4570 (in state); 1-800-541-WASH.

Increasingly sophisticated,
the city still guards its close
ties to the great outdoors

The City

Ask one group of Seattleites what the city is all about and they will say Boeing, football, and fishing. Ask the same question of the neighbors and the response will be opera and sailing. A good many other answers would also be correct, for this northwesternmost of large United States cities (about 500,000 within incorporated limits; 1.6 million in the greater Seattle area) is remarkable for both outdoor and indoor attractions.

Seattle fits tightly between a lake and an inland sea, and a bit more loosely between two towering mountain ranges. In the long twilights of summer, boats by the thousands move easily on calm water until 9 P.M. or even later. In winter, office workers escape after the workday to any of several areas to ski away their cares on lighted slopes, with a mere hour's drive the price of being there.

For a long time this benign outdoors overwhelmed most would-be urbanity. In the early 1960s a tightly knit colony of painters flourished in the city, but sold its canvases elsewhere. A slim but steady stream of jazz musicians had called Seattle home between road trips since the 1940s. The Seattle Symphony enjoyed a quiet reputation for excellence, but only enough listeners to support a short season.

However, with the World's Fair of 1962 came a blossoming of the arts. The first great sign was in 1970, when the now famous Seattle Opera Company outdrew the now infamous Seattle Pilots baseball team for a whole season.

The pace of life in the city has quickened with each passing year. A whole new skyline is visible from the World Fair's Space Needle. The Smith Tower, for decades trumpeted to all comers as the tallest building west of the Mississippi, is now just the tallest building on its block. (The Columbia Tower claims the tallest building honors.) Seattle has become a fine city for viewing films, browsing through books, and enjoying gourmet desserts, yet the city is still well wedded to its great outdoors. The combination is most attractive.

Weather. Outsiders are pleased to tell other outsiders that Seattle's principal product is rain. In sheer volume, the rain is not so impressive. The annual average is 34 inches; however, the modest total spreads itself around. In a typical year, Seattle accepts measurable precipitation on 152 days. As the figures hint, only a few howling storms come along each winter. Most Seattle rain falls too softly to interfere with gardening, golfing, weekend sailing, or bicycling.

Almost all Seattle weather is as temperate as its rainfall. The temperature crests into the 90° F. range only about twice each summer, while the average winter's maximum fails to reach 32° on just two days. (Overnight frosts occur an average of 15 times downtown, 40 in the open suburbs.)

There is a dry season. When the year lives up to the averages, only five July days see rain, and only six in August. Between them, these two months have 22 of the city's annual ration of 71 cloudless days.

Winter visitors must know that it can snow. Seattle, all hills, gets its snow wet. When packed it becomes slippery; a great many cars are left in awkward places by demoralized owners.

Highways. Interstate Highway 5 slices Seattle in half along its long, skinny north-south axis. The freeway is nonstop except during the rush hours. Beyond all doubt I-5 is the most efficient way into the city from Vancouver, British Columbia, to the north, or Portland, Oregon, to the south.

Approaching Seattle from the east, Interstate 90 is freeway across Mercer Island and on the Lacey B. Murrow (Mercer Island) Floating Bridge. Just north, the Evergreen Point Floating Bridge (State 520) spans Puget Sound, linking I-5 and I-405.

From the Seattle-Tacoma International Airport (Sea-Tac), I-405 cuts east to an intersection with I-5 for traffic bound downtown. I-405 then loops around the east side of Lake Washington, rejoining I-5 some miles north of the city. This route is a good bypass for anyone wishing to avoid congestion on the downtown stretches of I-5. Fast, frequent bus service on I-405 and I-5 links the airport with a downtown terminal at Sixth Avenue and Seneca Street.

Aside from these interstate freeways, Seattle has few expressways. For north-south traffic, old U.S.

# of Seattle

See additional maps on pages 12 and 28.

Highway 99 (now State Highway 99) can be a useful alternative to I-5. It is called Marginal Way in the industrial south end of the city, the Alaskan Way Viaduct in midcity, and Aurora Avenue in the residential-commercial north end.

Crosstown traffic gets along on arterial streets. The downtown area is a grid of one-way streets.

The city and all of sprawling King County are served by a unified bus system, Metro Transit, that not only serves the downtown area, but has routes leading well into the Cascades.

Accommodations. Seattle's major hotels cluster together on or close to Fifth Avenue in the main shopping district. To the north, between that district and the Seattle Center—site of the 1962 Seattle World's Fair—are several sizable motels. Smaller, more modest motels string out still farther to the north along Aurora Avenue. The largest of Seattle's motels—several of them—flank Seattle-Tacoma International Airport on old U.S. 99. Suburban Bellevue has the only other sizable cluster of hostelries, all near exits from I-405.

But this does not exhaust the list by any means. One large, luxury motel perches on a waterfront pier. The University of Washington district has a large hotel and several smaller motels. And bed and breakfast accommodations are sprinkled throughout Seattle's neighborhoods.

The Urban Core

Although Seattle stretches almost 20 miles south to north, its urban attractions cluster together in a remarkably compact core area.

The center of the business and downtown shopping district can be placed at Fifth Avenue and Pine Street. Major hotels and fine restaurants are within 5 blocks. Many of the city's luxury shops are on Fifth, or just off it.

From Fifth and Pine, the Seattle Center is but 9 blocks north (and brought closer by the nonstop, 60-cents-a-ride monorail connecting the two points). Revitalized Pioneer Square and the bulky

Kingdome are only 12 and 17 blocks south, respectively. The lively Pike Place Market lies a mere 5 blocks west; the waterfront is just below it.

Most of downtown is served by Metro Transit buses. In the Free Ride area, all riders board free. Those who debark within the Free Ride Area pay nothing. The boundaries are Battery and South Jackson streets, the waterfront, and Sixth Avenue.

The Seattle Center

The concrete reminders of Expo 1962 clustering on the original 74-acre site just north of the main business district are still a major urban attraction.

The emblem of the fair, the Space Needle, has a lofty observation deck 520 feet above the ground and a revolving restaurant almost as high. Both are reached by a high-speed toll elevator.

The Pacific Science Center, notable for its airy arches and courtyard, houses both a special-effects theater and a hands-on museum. Many of the permanent exhibits cover technology, but there is also a reconstructed Northwest Indian longhouse. A special area is geared to children.

The Seattle Art Museum Pavilion offers changing exhibits.

The Center House features multicultural fast food, souvenir shops, and, often, entertainment—reverberating through a three-story space. Downstairs is the Children's Museum; upstairs and down a passageway is the Pacific Arts Center.

Other buildings include the Coliseum (mainly for trade shows and popular concerts), the Opera House, the Bagley Wright Theater, and the Arena.

The Fun Forest amusement park near the Center House offers games and rides.

The handsomely landscaped grounds hold several heroic fountains—beautiful in any weather but especially heartening in the rain, when they give Seattleites a definite sense of fighting back.

Seattle Center maintains a listing of the numerous events scheduled on the grounds; call (206) 625-5404. For a guided tour of the Center, call (206) 625-2206.

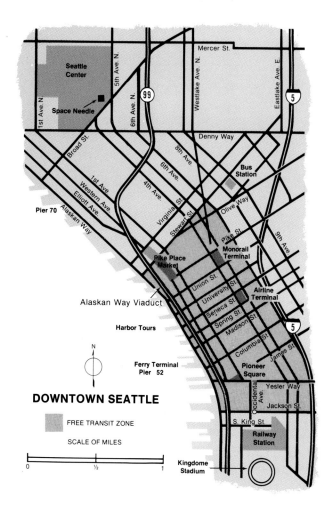

DOWNTOWN SEATTLE

FREE TRANSIT ZONE

SCALE OF MILES

0   ½   1

Pike Place Market

Slowly but inevitably, Seattle's Pike Place Market is changing. From its founding in 1907 through the 1950s, it was a classic street market after the European model. Scores of farmers from truck gardens in the rich river valleys south of town rented stalls at 25 cents a day at the foot of Pike Street and sold fresh produce to downtown office workers. Fish and meat markets added their wares. A handful of offbeat restaurants fed the farmers and their customers from dawn through the lunch hour. A sparse scattering of secondhand stores filled in the nooks and crannies.

Now the truck gardens are nearly all gone, replaced by suburban housing. The main market building is part produce market, part flea market, and part arts and crafts fair. Other buildings facing the market contain sophisticated shops, all handsomely housed because of a thoughtful renewal project for the whole district.

Though things aren't what they used to be, the rambling market building remains a good place for kids to find out about unusual vegetables and meats, as well as some of the more curious edibles from the sea. Its maze of ramps and stairs makes it a great place for losing mothers for a while.

Like the Seattle Center, the market was planned for the rainy climate. You can explore for hours under a single roof, and for hours more under another roof just across the street.

Linking the market with the waterfront is the Pike Place Hill Climb—flights of stairs (and elevators) that descend from market level to sea level.

The market is at Pike Street just off First Avenue.

The Waterfront

Seattle, like San Francisco, has two waterfronts: the old one, built for the smaller ships of an earlier day, is turning into a superior recreational resource, while the newer, working waterfront hides away farther from the visitor's city (its huge orange cranes lift containers from ship to pier; they are visible south of the tourist area).

Seattle's recreational waterfront stretches from Pier 48 to Pier 70—roughly from the lower end of the main business district north to the top end. It is less than a mile from the major downtown hotels. The stroll from one end to the other offers diverse charms in a short distance.

Pier 48 belongs to the Alaska Ferries. The information office there provides arrival and departure schedules. (Don't assume that you can buy passage on a whim; advance reservations are required.) A park dedicated to Alaska fronts the pier.

Next door, at the foot of Washington Street, is a public boat landing.

On Pier 51, Ye Olde Curiosity Shop bulges with souvenirs. It also has museum-quality Indian and Eskimo art and artifacts.

The Washington State Ferries have their headquarters at Pier 52, which is also the dock for the Bremerton and Bainbridge Island runs. (For a complete roster of ferry routes, see page 36.)

Next to the ferry terminal is Firehouse 5, home to Seattle's fireboats.

Pier 54 houses indoor and outdoor eateries (outdoors, sea gulls beg to share the fish and chips).

Pier 55 contains shops and is also the home dock for tour and charter boats. In addition to harbor tours, visits are offered to Blake Island's Tillicum Village, where an Indian-style salmon bake and traditional dancing are the main attractions.

Most of Pier 56 is taken up by a large import store; there are also a couple of restaurants.

Pier 57 is a waterfront park and public fishing pier. The deck has holes cut into it for drop-line artists. Benches and picnic tables make this an excellent point to tarry. You'll also find a number of specialty shops and restaurants.

Salmon . . . King of Washington's Sport Fish

The salmon in all its varieties is one of nature's great enigmas, and in most of those varieties is one of the most delicious fish in the world.

The salmon is anadromous, which is to say it spawns in fresh water but swims most of its adult life in salt water. That is not so uncommon. However, the Pacific salmon virtually disappears from the time it hatches and drifts down to the sea to the time it returns—2 to 5 years later—as an adult fish ready to spawn in its turn. It is known that the schools swim vast distances, but the exact routes are unknown.

The other peculiarity of this fish is that it spawns only once, inevitably dying as the concluding gesture of spawning. Salmon born in a natural stream choose the exact place of their birth when they spawn. How salmon find their own birthplace is not known exactly, but it appears to have some relationship to the exact chemical composition of the home water. They seem to smell their way home. Hatchery fish can be observed trying to swim into the inlet pipes that bring water into the pond where they hatched.

Five species are commonly found in Washington waters. They are known to science by their common Russian names. *Orcorhynchus tschawytscha* is the great Chinook (also known as king, tyee, spring, and quinnat). This is the largest of salmon, averaging 20 pounds but capable of thrice that weight. The other great edible salmon is *O. kisutch*, better known as the silver or coho. In addition to these there are the pink (also called the humpie), the sockeye (also called red), and chum (also called dog salmon because the Indians of old reserved it for dog food). Fishermen also refer to the blackmouth, but it is an immature Chinook.

The great seasons for fishermen are spring, summer, and fall, when the fish gather from all across the Pacific for their annual spawning runs up dozens of rivers, especially the Columbia. However, man is spreading the season out to a year-round one through unseasonal releases of hatchery-raised fish that do not follow the migratory patterns of fish released in the natural cycle, but stay in Puget Sound.

Inland saltwater areas east of the entrance to the Strait of Juan de Fuca are open to fishing the year around. The sheltered waters are calm even in winter. From November through April, schools of salmon mill around and feed in the areas around the Strait, the San Juan Islands, and Puget Sound, including Hood Canal and Elliott Bay directly in front of Seattle.

Both Chinook and coho are in these regions in winter. Typically, their weights range from a couple of pounds for coho and yearling Chinooks up to 20 pounds for 4th-year Chinooks.

Outside the Strait and along the Pacific Coast of Washington, the ocean season begins in early July and extends through August.

The great summer runs of spawning fish bring coho in the 4- and 5-pound range and Chinooks weighing as much as 40 pounds. (Once in a while, someone brings in a giant Chinook at 60 or even 70 pounds.)

Westport and Ilwaco are the two great ports for charter boats working the Columbia River runs. Upcoast, small charter fleets operate at Neah Bay, Sekiu, and Port Angeles. These latter also offer small rental boats called kickers for near-shore fishing.

Inside Puget Sound there are few charter boats, but many opportunities to rent kickers. Particularly active spots are Ballard and West Seattle in Seattle, Hansville on the Kitsap Peninsula, Anacortes, and the San Juan resorts. Most of the shoreside cities north of Seattle on Puget Sound have at least one marina with rental boats.

Day-trip charters run from $40 to $50 per person, with rental gear available for a small extra charge. Kickers with outboards usually rent for $25 a day, give or take a few dollars.

Washington does require a license for salmon, and anglers must have a salmon punch card (obtainable at most sporting goods stores and marinas) in their possession.

Bag limits and seasonal closures of waters are strictly enforced. Also, there are some underwater marine parks closed to fishing at all times. Any angler should have a current copy of *Sportfishing Regulations for Salmon, Shellfish and Bottomfish*, available along with punch cards or by writing the Washington Department of Fisheries, 115 General Administration Building, Olympia, WA 98504.

Salmon also may be taken in certain freshwater lakes and streams; the seasonal closures and boundaries of these are quite complex, but are described in the pamphlet.

Next door, Pier 59 houses the Aquarium, the Omnidome Theater, and the Museum of Sea and Ships. The Aquarium has both indoor and outdoor exhibits designed to expose people to fish in their natural habitat. Hours are 10 A.M. to 7 P.M. daily from Memorial Day to Labor Day, and 10 A.M. to 5 P.M. daily the rest of the year. The Omnidome shows several films a day on its 100-foot-high, 180-degree curved dome screen. The Museum of Sea and Ships is a unique collection of ancient and modern equipment and ships.

After a spate of working piers comes a large inn built partly over the water on piers 67 and 68. Pier 69 is headquarters of the *Princess Marguerite* and the *Vancouver Island Princess*, the British Columbia Steamship Company's day boats to Canada and back. The same pier is home to the *Victoria Clipper*, a passengers-only çatamaran that speeds to Victoria in 2½ hours. It operates daily, year-round.

Pier 70, the most northerly of the publicly accessible piers, is a complex of specialty shops and restaurants at the foot of Elliott Avenue. A large metered parking area adjoins the pier. Beyond it, the footpath and bike trail of Myrtle Edwards Park follow the waterfront north.

A large metered parking area adjoins Pier 70. Metered parking is also available all along the waterfront beneath the Alaskan Way Viaduct. Pier 70 has garage parking. All these areas are not enough on a fine summer's day, but the walk from town is not far for anyone in reasonably good physical condition.

To ease parking and walking woes, Metro Transit runs old-fashioned streetcars along the waterfront from Pioneer Square north to Myrtle Edwards Park. Passengers can get on and off at any of several stops along the way with transfers from the streetcars or any connecting Metro bus line. Transfers are valid for 90 minutes.

Pioneer Square: History Revived

Pioneer Square was the heart of Seattle in its rowdiest days—the era of the Alaska Gold Rush.

The fledgling city began to grow on that spot much earlier, when Henry Yesler's mill gave rise

New heights downtown

Like the mountains that surround it, the Seattle skyline rises high. In the foreground is the Space Needle, distinctive symbol of the 1962 World's Fair. Actually taller than the Space Needle, the dark building just to the right of it is the Columbia Tower. Both buildings have high observation areas that are open to visitors.

to the original definition of "skid road": a road on which logs were skidded to a mill. With the gold rush, Pioneer Square grew into the sort of place where a political quarrel could be settled on the street with pistols and where a great vaudeville circuit—the Pantages—would be born.

As a new, more sober city center emerged uptown, Pioneer Square developed the secondary, more durable definition of "skid road": a quarter for derelicts.

But today, after a long, drab interim, the ornate buildings are full of life again. Though by gentler modern definition there is still rowdiness at times, the main purposes of contemporary Pioneer Square are distinctive shopping, gallery-hopping, and eating. Nearly 100 businesses belong to the Pioneer Square Association, with restaurants leading in numbers.

The quarter encompasses the 12 square blocks from the waterfront east to Second Avenue, and from South King Street north to Yesler Way. Bits and pieces lap over those boundaries, however, especially on the north. A map showing the location of each member firm in the association is available in most shops in the quarter.

One bit of the old days still remains, though it cannot accurately be said to live. The original buildings were built in a boggy spot, and the current streets and structures were simply added on top of the old. Some of the musty, dusty originals can now be seen on a private tour called Seattle Underground. Tours depart from Doc Maynard's Public House, which faces into Pioneer Square proper from First Avenue and Yesler Way. The guides provide a witty, literate history of old Seattle as they lead groups through the dim caverns of another era. There is a charge.

One other touch of nostalgia may be found in the Western Union office at South Main Street and Occidental Avenue, where old-fashioned and brand-new pieces of equipment are on display in the lobby. Would-be telegraphers can have a go at Morse code on a sending key.

Klondike Gold Rush National Historical Park, at 117 South Main, recalls turn-of-the-century days of gold-seeking mania. It is open daily.

The Pioneer Square region is attractive the year around, but notably so in summer, when several sidewalk cafes blossom. Pioneer Square itself is a small park—combining a wrought-iron pergola and a totem pole—at First Avenue and Yesler Way. A larger, cobble-paved park runs 2 blocks along Occidental Avenue, from South Washington Street to South Jackson.

The Kingdome

For major events, as many as 64,000 people crowd into the King County Domed Stadium, or, as it is more commonly called, the Kingdome. But even when nothing is going on, the giant stadium on the south edge of the Pioneer Square district attracts a considerable flow of visitors.

The management runs tours daily, unless events conflict. For a modest fee, the 45-minute tour rambles through the structure, then pauses for a leisurely look at a sports museum.

The International District

Officially it is called the International District—and occasionally Chinatown. By whatever name, the area just east of the Kingdome—from Sixth Avenue South to Eighth Avenue, and from Yesler Way to Lane Street—is home to people from many cultures across the Pacific.

Within these few blocks a diligent looker can find cultural centers, excellent ethnic eating, a fortune cooky factory, martial arts emporiums, import shops filled with Asian goods, and an herbalist or two.

An introductory slide show and self-guiding map of the area are available at the Nippon Kan Theater, 628 South Washington Street. The ticket costs $2.00. For the required reservation, call (206) 624-6342 or write (the ZIP is 98104).

The Nippon Kan Theater, a national historic site, offers varied entertainment. For a listing of events in the theater, call (206) 624-8800.

The terraces of a community garden step down the hillside from the Nippon Kan Theater.

Of particular note in the district are the Wing Luke Museum and Northwest Asian American Theater at 407 7th Avenue South. Here are presented Asian folk art, calligraphy, photography, artifacts, and changing exhibits. For current information, phone (206) 623-5124.

The glamorous red-and-gold pavilion in Hing Hay Park, at the corner of South King Street and Maynard Avenue South, was a gift from Taiwan.

Freeway Park

The last of Seattle's central city attractions is pure oasis: a park built across the top of Interstate 5.

Technically, the park is a huge concrete and steel machine, complete with piping systems that deliver irrigation water and nutrients to plants, pump and recirculate fountain waters, and drain away rainwater.

Practically, it is a walker's park, a viewer's park, and a picnicker's park. In summer, it's also a music appreciation park, with the Out to Lunch series of summer concerts.

A concrete canyon holds a torrential waterfall that drowns out traffic noise. Within concrete retaining walls, trees give shade and lawns give repose. An area of plants in concrete walls—called

the Great Box Garden—lies between Sixth and Seventh avenues and between Spring and Seneca streets. The canyon and waterfall is between Seventh and Eighth, and between Seneca and University. A big lawn and children's play area flank the freeway east of Eighth.

The whole park—5.7 acres—lies close to major hotels, the convention center, and the heart of Seattle's downtown shopping district.

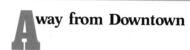

Away from Downtown

By and large, Seattle lacks exotic neighborhoods. One exception—the International District—has already been noted. The only other ethnic enclave is predominantly Scandinavian Ballard, in the northwest quarter of the city.

Though perhaps not exotic, Seattle's neighborhoods are distinctive and inspire strong loyalty among their residents. Three of the most noteworthy are the houseboat moorages on Lake Union (best seen from the water), the bright lights of Broadway on Capitol Hill, and the residential areas along the Lake Washington shoreline. Queen Ann Hill, Magnolia, Fremont, West Seattle, and Wallingford—among others—are like villages within the city.

The University of Washington

Of the three universities within the city, only the University of Washington has created its own distinctive neighborhood.

Like all great university campuses—and this one has one of the largest enrollments of any single campus in the country, some 34,000 students—the University of Washington offers a number of subtle, understated attractions for visitors, not to mention the fiercer joys of a full schedule of Pac-10 athletics.

The sprawling campus is bounded on the south by the Lake Washington Ship Canal (Montlake Cut), on the east by the lake itself, and on the north by NE 45th Street. The western boundary changes from 15th Avenue NE to 11th Avenue NE; the campus is just a few blocks east of I-5.

Old grads seeking to stroll down memory lane will find their progress oft impeded by buildings they do not remember. Large expanses of onetime lawn have given way to new halls. Still, this campus remains beautiful enough and architecturally interesting enough to merit a leisurely stroll before or after a visit to some specific attraction.

A visitor center at NE Campus Parkway and University Way NE will furnish information (operating hours of museums, calendars of events) and a walker's map. Some public parking is available in the northwest corner of campus, at the 17th Avenue entrance off NE 45th Street.

In the northwest corner of the campus, the Thomas Burke Memorial-Washington State Museum focuses upon men and beasts of the Pacific Rim and the often shaky ground they live on. Exhibits combining zoology and geology reach back in time to the age of dinosaurs. The view of humanity is not as long but emphasizes early times.

Henry Art Gallery, located on the campus at the corner of NE 41st Street and 15th Avenue NE, houses a permanent collection of turn-of-the-century paintings donated by the philanthropist for whom the museum is named. Its schedule of special loans and exhibitions encompasses contemporary and historical works of art representative of many times and many places.

University of Washington student actors have three stages on which to perform. The Penthouse, the first theater-in-the-round in the United States, is still in regular use. One block off campus at NE 40th and University Way NE is the University's Glenn Hughes Playhouse, a thrust-stage theater. Meany Hall for the Performing Arts is located on "Red Square," a brick plaza. Meany is also the site of performances by professional in-city and touring companies.

Of interest elsewhere on campus are a pharmaceutical garden (see page 24) and the athletic plant (see page 21).

One block west of campus, University Way NE runs parallel to the west boundary. From NE 42nd Street north to NE 47th Street, "the Ave" and its cross streets are the commercial center and one of the social centers of student life. Here is a useful observation point for the latest youthful fashions in clothing, food, music, and movies. The array of new and used bookstores is unequaled in a single neighborhood elsewhere in the city.

Chittenden Locks

An important link in the chain of waterways that makes Seattle such a fine boating city, the locks connect freshwater Lake Washington and Lake Union with saltwater Puget Sound.

At 825 feet long by 80 feet wide, and with a maximum lift of 26 feet, Chittenden handles an astonishing 78,000 vessels each year. For sheer numbers of boats and intensity of action, late afternoon on a summer weekend is the time to go. Lock-keepers load the huge concrete trough as full as they can get it of everything from outboards to regal schooners for each operation of the locks. A good day's work is 1,200 vessels.

Visitors can look directly down into the locks from either side or from walkways across the tops of the lock gates themselves. Those who would live the experience can find rental boats at several locations.

On the south side of the locks is a fish ladder, through which highly visible salmon runs pass each fall and winter en route to spawning grounds in fresh water.

Also on the locks' grounds is a seven-acre collection of exotic plants, the Carl S. English Jr. Ornamental Gardens (see page 24).

NW Market Street leads through Ballard to a parking lot at the main entrance to the grounds. Admission is free. For information, call (206) 783-7059.

Woodland Park Zoo and Green Lake

Two of Seattle's primary recreation resources, Woodland Park and Green Lake, adjoin—although seeing all of both areas in one visit would be a very tiring undertaking.

A 90-acre zoo is the main attraction of Woodland Park. The African Savanna is an open five-acre natural habitat with free-roaming giraffes, zebras, and (in a separate area) lions. The zoo's gorillas also have a comfortable home. The Nocturnal House offers a rare opportunity to observe night creatures from all over the world. At the Family Farm, children can join in all sorts of farm-related activities. For complete information on hours, exhibits, and activities, write 5500 Phinney Avenue North, Seattle, WA 98103, or call (206) 789-7919.

Within the spacious confines of the park are abundant picnic grounds and courts and fields for all manner of games. Just across from the elegant rose garden at the main entrance to the park is the Poncho Theater, home of the Seattle Children's Theater.

The park straddles Aurora Avenue between North 50th and North 59th streets. The zoo and rose gardens are in upper Woodland, west of Aurora. The picnic areas and sports fields are in lower Woodland, east of Aurora. Green Lake flanks lower Woodland.

Green Lake offers swimming beaches, a swimming pool, rental boats, the Bathhouse Theater, playgrounds, fishing piers, and the city's most popular jogging and bicycling path.

Scattered Points of Interest

Seattle's suburbs and nearby communities offer a number of small enchantments, often one of a kind. Here they are listed from south of the city to north of it.

Seattle-Tacoma International Airport (Sea-Tac), like most modern metropolitan airports, has developed a world of its own. The terminal has given rise to a ring of major motels, restaurants, and other amenities for travelers. A sizable residential population nearby has produced a large shopping mall—Southcenter—about 3 miles from the airport.

The terminal itself contains a permanent collection of artworks in media ranging from sculpture to light-and-sound. The airport also has a meditation room, a peaceful refuge from page calls and canned music. Last, there is an automated subway train linking the terminals.

Sea-Tac flanks Pacific Highway South between South 154th Street and South 188th Street. Directions are clearly marked to and from I-5.

The Museum of Flight, near the Boeing aerospace plant south of downtown, presents the history of aviation technology in The Red Barn, the original home of the Boeing Aerospace Company, and the six-story glass-and-steel Great Gallery. Exhibits include full-size aircraft. Open daily in summer, closed Mondays the rest of the year, the museum is just off I-5 at 9404 East Marginal Way South.

The Rainier Brewery, maker of distinctive fermented beverages, is open for tours and tasting daily during business hours. The brewery is in the industrial south end of Seattle, at 3100 Airport Way South. (Airport Way South parallels Interstate 5; the brewery is near Exit 163A.)

Chateau Ste. Michelle faithfully re-creates the facade of a French wine chateau. Behind the facade lies an up-to-date winemaking facility, Washington's largest and one of its most prestigious. A well-planned tour explains every step of winemaking, from picking grapes to corking bottles. The last stop is a tasting room. Tours run daily during business hours.

The winery is near the town of Woodinville, northeast of Seattle. The simplest route is I-405 to the State 522 exit, east less than a mile on 522 to the Woodinville exit, then south for slightly more than a mile on State 202.

Museums and the Arts

Seattle is no longer the city Sir Thomas Beecham so confidently called a "cultural dustbin." Seattle has built a substantial community of artists, both visual and performing.

The Arts Hotline (447-ARTS) provides up-to-the-minute information on nonprofit arts organizations in the Seattle area, including film and video, children's events, free events, and literary readings.

Historic and Cultural Museums

Specialized museums, large and small, enrich the city.

The Museum of History and Industry, near the University of Washington campus, is just off Montlake Boulevard on the south side of the Lake Washington Ship Canal (popularly known as the Montlake Cut). It harbors diverse reminders of Seattle history, from the tools of pioneer doctors to a hydroplane. The information number is (206) 324-1125.

Just inside the 45th and 17th Street entrance to the University of Washington campus, the Burke Museum concentrates on anthropology, geology and zoology. Outside the entrance is a garden of native plants. The attractively designed building provides a spacious, airy display space, while the cafe downstairs has an old-world feeling. For information call (206) 543-5590.

The Nordic Heritage Museum in Ballard features Scandinavian memorabilia. For directions, call (206) 789-5707.

The Wing Luke Memorial Museum in the International District portrays the history of Seattle's Asian community along with Asian folk art and crafts. For current hours, write 414 8th Ave. S., Seattle, WA 98104, or call (206) 623-5124.

Art Museums and Galleries

The Seattle Art Museum, in Volunteer Park at the top of Capitol Hill (14th Avenue East and East Prospect), displays permanent collections of European masters, contemporary art, and Asian art. The jade gallery is a popular attraction, as are the African exhibits and the traveling exhibitions.

The Seattle Art Museum Pavilion, in Seattle Center, houses traveling exhibitions of many types. For more information about either of the Seattle Art Museum's centers, call (206) 443-4670.

Frye Art Museum, 704 Terry Avenue, (206) 622-9250, contains the collection of 18th- and 19th-century European and American paintings gathered and donated by Charles and Emma Frye. Its permanent collection includes fine arts and crafts of the greater northwest.

In addition to these centers, the Henry Art Gallery on the University of Washington campus, (206) 543-2280, displays fine art exhibits.

The Center on Contemporary Art (COCA) sponsors exhibits in various locations. For more information, call the Arts Hotline (447-ARTS).

The largest group of galleries in the city is in the Pioneer Square area.

Music

From old-world opera to avant-garde jazz, music lovers can hear their own sort of tune in this city.

Food and shelter

*Silvery salmon, fresh-cooked shrimp—
the bounty of land and sea (left) fills
the bins at the Pike Place Market.
Originally strictly a marketplace, the
area has grown into a dynamic living-
shopping-working neighborhood.
Pioneer Square (below), the business
heart of early Seattle, has also enjoyed
extensive rehabilitation and preservation. Its revitalized brick buildings
exist side-by-side with new offices and
dwelling places.*

Washington's Clams

One good thing about clams is steaming them in a bucket over a beach fire, dipping them in butter, and eating them right there. Another good thing, with larger species, is canning ground clam meat for thick, steaming winter-night chowders. But one of the best things about clams is digging them.

Clam digging on Washington's sheltered beaches is a vigorous but safe exercise for a loner, a picnic crowd, or a family. There are enough different kinds of clams on enough different kinds of beaches to guarantee some digging to anyone who can get to a representative strip of saltwater beach.

The equipment consists of a gunny sack or other carrying device and a rake, hoe, trowel, shovel, or clam gun—depending on the species sought. The clam gun, a specialty device for capturing razor clams, is a metal cylinder on the end of a handle. A caisson—a metal ring to shore up the sides of a deep hole while digging—may prove useful. A change of clothes for later is a good idea, as are waterproof shoes or boots when it's cold.

All digging is most productive on minus tides, from 2 hours before low tide to 2 hours after.

Although Washington does not require a license for shellfish, the state does impose bag limits. Also, some areas are seasonal, due to possible red tide poisoning, gill parasites, and population worries. Check with the Washington Department of Fisheries, 115 General Administration Building, Olympia, WA 98504. Telephone 1-800-562-5672.

The following is a roster of commonly dug clams from Puget Sound and the Strait of Juan de Fuca, and also Grays and Willapa harbors.

Bent-nosed clam. Averaging 2 inches across, it is tough, and often can be found where other varieties cannot endure. It inhabits muddy bays. It can be raked out or dug with shovels. Most are found at a 6- to 8-inch depth. The meat has a good flavor; use it whole in bouillabaisse or other stews, or chopped in chowder. (If used whole, it needs 2 days in salt water to flush mud from its stomach.)

Gaper clam. More commonly known as the horse clam or horseneck in the Northwest, it weighs as much as 3 pounds. It lives in firm, clean bay sand, usually at a depth of 2 feet or more. Its long siphon can retract quickly from the surface, giving the impression that it is digging down. It must be dug with a shovel. In wet sand a caisson may be needed to shore up the edges of a hole long enough to get down to the shell. The siphon is the edible part; its tough layer of skin must be peeled away before cooking. Most people grind or dice the meat.

Geoduck. (pronounced *gooey-duck*). Largest of Washington's clams, it ranges from a modest 3 pounds up to a record 10. It lives in muddy bay bottoms, frequently near or in eel grass, at depths ranging to 3 feet. Like the gaper, it retracts a long siphon when disturbed. Holes must be supported by caissons. The meat is much like that of the gaper.

Razor. Washington's great coastal clam boasts a sporting chance of making a getaway unless pursued with skill. Try driving a shovel straight into the sand 6 inches on the seaward side of the "show" (the dime-size dimple around the siphon), taking a couple of quick scoops underneath and toward the clam, then grabbing for the quarry.

Rock cockle. Ranging up to 2 inches across, it lives in bays all along the coast, frequently near the mouth, usually in gravel. It lives at a depth of 2 to 8 inches. Rakes work in fine gravel; trowels are useful where gravel mixes with larger rock. This is the steamed clam of northwest restaurants, and that is the way it tastes best. Locally it is sometimes known as the littleneck.

Softshell clam. It burrows in muddy bays—ones still enough for the tideflats to be malodorous. The clam must be dug with gentle horizontal swipes of a shovel to avoid crushing the delicate shell. It is a clam for stews, requiring cleaning and skinning to be pleasant in flavor.

Washington clam. Also called the Martha Washington, this sweet-meated clam grows to 5 inches across, lives in slightly muddier sand than the gaper (see at left) at a depth of 8 inches or slightly more. It is most efficiently dug with a shovel. The meat is tasty enough to steam, but the slick texture causes it to be more likable in chowders or other stews.

The Department of Fisheries (see at left) offers a fine set of maps showing publicly accessible Puget Sound beaches and their possible edibles (clams, oysters, crabs, etc.).

The Seattle Opera Association maintains a regular season from September through May. In August, the company produces two complete cycles of Wagner's Ring. All performances take place in the Opera House at the Seattle Center. For information, write P.O. Box 9248, Seattle, WA 98109. Telephone (206) 443-4700.

The Seattle Symphony performs its annual series of concerts in the Seattle Center Opera House and in a number of other locations. For years the symphony has enjoyed a fine reputation (and recording contracts) as a polished orchestra. For information: 305 Harrison Street, Seattle, WA 98109. Telephone for general information: (206) 443-4740; for tickets: (206) 443-4747.

The Early Music Guild, (206) 325-7066, and the Ladies Musical Club, (206) 525-7889, are among the groups sponsoring performances.

The city's universities and colleges, particularly the University of Washington, offer active schedules of music by groups ranging from string quartets to symphony orchestras. The University of Washington information number is (206) 543-4880.

Classic and symphonic music aside, Seattle also has a long friendship with jazz. Check the current newspaper listings for information on who's playing at the various clubs.

Theater and Dance

Seattle is especially rich in theater. It supports several full-time acting companies and a large pool of talent. Any time of year, there are a number of lively productions to choose from. Dance is represented by visiting companies and the Pacific Northwest Ballet, Seattle's classic dance mainstay.

Seattle Repertory Theater, the city's most well-known professional theater company, performs classic, contemporary, and new works in the Bagley Wright Theater on the Seattle Center grounds. Its season is mid-October through mid-May. For information: 155 Mercer Street, Seattle, WA 98109; (206) 443-2222.

A Contemporary Theater (ACT) presents its season in a theater near the Seattle Center grounds. The location of the theater and source of ticket information is 100 West Roy Street, Seattle, WA 98119. Telephone: (206) 285-5110.

The Bathhouse Theater company performs year-round, with its official season from March through December. Most performances are in its own theater, at 7312 W. Greenlake Drive North, (206) 524-9108.

Two other active theater groups in the city are the Empty Space, (206) 467-6000; and Intiman, (206) 624-2992. Pioneer Square, New City, and University of Washington Drama also offer exciting performances. Young ACT Theater and the Seattle Children's Theater perform for younger theatergoers.

Pacific Northwest Ballet is the prima dance group. It attained new recognition when it commissioned Maurice Sendak to design the sets for a new production of *Nutcracker*. Most performances are held in the Opera House at Seattle Center. For complete information, call (206) 443-4751.

Spectator Sports

After years of living or dying with the University of Washington Huskies, Seattle has recently acquired a number of professional franchises to spread the living and dying around. The city has also acquired a comfortable domed stadium.

On game day, tickets for any sport can be hard to come by.

The National Basketball Association's Seattle SuperSonics play their home schedule in the Kingdome on the south edge of the main business district. For more information: 419 Occidental Avenue South, Seattle, WA 98104. Telephone: (206) 628-8448.

The National Football League's Seattle Seahawks also play in the Kingdome. Mailing address is 5305 Lake Washington Boulevard, Kirkland, WA 98033. Telephone: (206) 827-9766.

The American League's Seattle Mariners play baseball in the Kingdome. Mailing address is P.O. Box 411, Seattle, WA 98104. Telephone: (206) 628-3300.

The other professional team in town is the Seattle Thunderbirds Hockey Club. They play in the Arena at the Seattle Center. For information on their schedule, call (206) 728-9124.

University of Washington athletic teams compete in the Pacific-10. The football stadium and basketball pavilion are adjacent to each other on the campus, along Montlake Boulevard just north of the Lake Washington Ship Canal. Mailing address is Intercollegiate Athletic Ticket Office, Tubby Graves Building, University of Washington, Seattle, WA 98105. Telephone: (206) 543-2200.

Seattle University's Chieftains basketball team plays its home games in a gym on campus. For information: Athletic Department, Seattle University, 550 Fourteenth Avenue, Seattle, WA 98112. Telephone: (206) 626-5305.

Finally, among the collegians, Seattle Pacific University's basketball teams compete effectively in the NCAA small schools division. The home court is on the Seattle Pacific campus, west of Lake Union. For information: Athletic Department, Seattle Pacific University, Third Avenue

West and West Nickerson, Seattle, WA 98119. Telephone: (206) 281-2085.

These schools also compete in spring sports. The most notable events are eight-oared crew races, in which Washington's Huskies are perennial power-houses. Baseball, track, and tennis are also scheduled by one or more of the three schools.

Longacres attracts good horses to its May-October season. Near Sea-Tac International, the handsome track is reached via Exit 154 from I-5, or Exit 1 from I-405.

Seattle Outdoors

Seattle does not have a great, all-in-one urban playground to compare with Vancouver's Stanley Park or Tacoma's Point Defiance. As a whole, however, Seattle's 5,000-acre system—consisting of 400 separate parks—has no match in the region. Coupled with nearby suburban municipal parks and the ranging King County system, Seattle's parks leave out virtually no type of terrain or outdoor activity.

Family Picnic Parks

Each corner of the city seems to have its own excellent picnic park with varied attractions for whole families. Two of the finest, Woodland Park and adjacent Green Lake, north of downtown, are described on page 17.

Discovery Park covers much of what used to be the Army's Fort Lawton, on Magnolia Bluff (enter at West Government Way and 36th Avenue West). Many of the fort's buildings are intact but boarded up. The grounds offer fine beach walks and nature trails. A fitness course, tennis courts, picnic areas, and an ideal kite-flying field are additional attractions. The visitor center number is (206) 625-4636. A lighthouse is open for tours on a regular basis; phone (206) 282-9130.

Also at the park is the Daybreak Star Indian Cultural Center, with art displays, meeting rooms, and distinctive landscaping; it's open daily.

Gasworks Park, on the north shore of Lake Union, might be the first choice of families with kids of grammar school age who need to blow off steam.

Stylish cap for a freeway

In an ingenious recapture of green space, Seattle built almost 6 acres of downtown park atop Interstate 5.

The park is literally an old gas works. Much of the old machinery has been cleaned and painted so children can crawl on, in, and through it. The gear is covered by a roof. So is a small cluster of picnic tables.

The park's other attraction is a fine kite hill, which looks right into the Seattle Police Department's busy heliport. (The hill is good for rolling down, too.) A sun dial sculpture tops the hill.

Gasworks is slightly more than a mile closer to downtown than Woodland Park–Green Lake, and almost a mile east of Aurora Boulevard.

Seward Park is Seattle's greatest recreational resource on Lake Washington. A peninsula, it has flat play lawns and swimming beaches at its base, but toward its outer end it is hilly and wooded. An expansive picnic area hides, serene, up in the woods. A trout hatchery within the park is open to visitors. The shoreline of the peninsula has pathways for walkers, joggers, and bicyclists. For the latter, a narrow band of lakeshore extends the possibilities 2 miles north, almost to the Lacey B. Murrow (Mercer Island) Floating Bridge. Lake Washington Boulevard provides access along the lake from either north or south.

Lincoln Park, in West Seattle, has saltwater beaches (and, for the less hardy, a heated saltwater pool), tree-shaded picnic grounds, and a variety of sports courts and fields. Somewhat remote from the rest of the city, Lincoln compensates with an atmosphere at once groomed and unspoiled. The beaches and a bluff above them are serene, more natural than not. The upper levels of the park are landscaped lawns dotted with mature trees.

From the Spokane Street access bridge into West Seattle, Fauntleroy Avenue extends directly to the front gate of the park.

Alki Beach Park. Also in West Seattle, the long beach from Alki Point to Duwamish Head supplements Lincoln Park's shore. This beach yields superb views across Elliott Bay to the downtown skyline and across Puget Sound to the Olympic Mountains. It is also the premier locale in town for beach fire picnics. Divers use the beach as a launch point for forays after diverse quarry, but especially the giant octopus.

A perimeter road around West Seattle hugs the backshore all the way.

Carkeek Park, on Puget Sound near the north city limits, has a beachfront much like Lincoln Park's, but the rest of Carkeek is essentially natural northwest woods. Many hikers use this park as a convenient short-notice retreat or conditioning ground.

Luther Burbank Park, headquarters of the King County system, occupies the northeastern tip of

Mercer Island. Most of its 77 acres remains in natural marsh-and-meadow state; amenities include day boat moorage, an amphitheater, a fishing pier, tennis courts, and a swimming beach. However, its finest feature for parents with grammar-school-age children is a play area of such imagination that it remains memorable to kids a year after they visit. To reach the park from I-90, exit on Island Crest Way.

Ed Munro Seahurst Park, a King County park, contains 4,000 feet of saltwater frontage on Puget Sound, south of the city limits near the community of Burien. Its sea wall is a favorite perch for fishermen. The park also has ample picnic grounds—the usual northwestern blend of open tables with barbecues and sheltered tables with cookstoves. Also on the 165-acre grounds are a teaching center dealing with marine biology and a fish ladder and holding pond.

The park is located in the vicinity of SW 144th Street. Access requires a detailed local map.

Saltwater State Park, farther south of Seattle along the Puget Sound shore, has much the same mixture of beach and picnic area, plus some campsites sheltered in trees well inshore. It is the closest state camping park to Seattle.

Parks Featuring Plants

Seattle's year-round mild climate lends itself to cultivation of a wide range of plants from around the world. Five major public gardens, all in a tidy row across the north end of town, invite thoughtful exploration by people who enjoy plants.

Volunteer Park features a conservatory and fine formal gardens surrounding the Seattle Art Museum. The park also has a water tower with a lofty viewing platform. Plaques on the platform identify principal peaks in both the Olympic and Cascade mountain ranges, and the perspective of the gardens below is a joy to the eye.

The main entrance is on 15th Avenue East at East Galer Street in the Capitol Hill district, south of the Lake Washington Ship Canal, east of I-5.

The Washington Park Arboretum is a great treasure trove for serious gardeners. The narrow park fronts on the Lake Washington Ship Canal just across from Husky Stadium, then runs more than a mile south across gently rolling terrain. Lake Washington Boulevard slips through the arboretum.

At the north end of a side road, Arboretum Drive East, is a visitor center.

The arboretum contains large collections of rhododendrons, azaleas, dogwoods, hollies, magnolias, crabapples, brooms, tree peonies, flowering cherries, and flowering quinces.

Next to Lake Washington Boulevard is a 4-acre Japanese tea garden. From spring through fall, the garden is open daily; it is closed from November through March. The modest admission fee goes toward maintenance.

For information about tours and events in the arboretum, call the visitor center at (206) 543-8800.

A nature trail extends from the Washington Park Arboretum out onto islands, then on a boardwalk through a marsh, and to the Museum of History and Industry (page 18).

A pharmaceutical garden, across the ship canal (also called the Montlake Cut) from the arboretum, on the main campus of the University of Washington, is filled with medicinal (and mostly toxic) plants such as foxglove, periwinkle, cascara, and horehound, plus such sweet-smelling plants as jasmine, lavender, and mint. The 2 acres of garden are between Frosh Pond (Drumheller Fountain) and the Medical School. For directions and a walking map, go to the University Visitors' Information Center at NE Campus Parkway and University Way NE.

The Center for Urban Horticulture isn't exactly a park, but it's an essential stop for plant enthusiasts. Operated by the University of Washington in a building on Union Bay Place, east of campus, it offers a myriad of plant-related activities to the public. For complete information, write University of Washington, GF-15, Seattle, WA 98195; telephone: (206) 545-8033.

Carl S. English Jr. Ornamental Gardens, at the Chittenden Locks (popularly known as the Ballard Locks), has a collection of well-labeled trees and shrubs on its grounds near the parking lot. Many of the specimens are Asian exotics gathered since 1940. A leaflet and guide map to the 7-acre garden are available at the gatehouse. The garden is open daily from 7 A.M. to 9 P.M. (For more information about the locks, see page 17.)

Woodland Park has an extensive collection of old-fashioned roses, along with many newer ones, in a garden just inside the gate at North 50th Street and Fremont Avenue, 2 blocks west of Aurora Avenue. (Also see page 17.)

Bicycling and Jogging

Seattle and the surrounding communities have done much to make life pleasant for both bicyclists and joggers, who usually share the same routes.

The most popular run-or-ride route in Seattle circles Green Lake. The fairly level, asphalted 3-mile track carries so much traffic that the park department painted a white line down the middle. Signs show which side is for whom.

Not far behind in popularity among joggers is the waterfront. Downtown office workers and hotel guests pick up the waterside walkway at a handy point and run north. Beyond the piers, grassy Myrtle Edwards Park extends the run almost 2 miles. (Why, nonjoggers may ask, bother to go down to the waterfront? Because, joggers respond, there are no signal lights or cross streets to break the rhythm.)

The Burke-Gilman hiking and bicycling trail starts at Gasworks Park, on the shore of Lake Union near the University of Washington campus, and runs generally northward all the way to King County's Logboom Park (in Kenmore, on the northeast corner of Lake Washington)—a jaunt of 12½ miles one-way in varied terrain. The surroundings range from shopping districts to open countryside. The Burke-Gilman Trail links to the Sammamish River Trail, which extends down the east side of Lake Washington from the town of Bothell to Marymoor County Park near Redmond. Marymoor also has a velodrome.

Somewhat farther from the central hotel area, Lake Washington Boulevard follows the lakeshore, mostly in parklike surroundings, for several miles from the Lake Washington Floating Bridge south to Seward Park. Although the route is popular with local runners, it is out of the way as a fitness course for visitors. The fine scenery recommends this route to cyclists.

Similarly, a marked and paved bicycle route rims West Seattle's Puget Sound shoreline for several miles around Duwamish Head and out to Alki Point. The marked trail ends there, but lightly traveled local streets make an extended ride to Lincoln Park enjoyable.

Tennis

Outdoor public tennis courts are scattered throughout Seattle: the city operates one sizable indoor tennis center. Across the lake in Bellevue is a public combination indoor/outdoor complex.

The Seattle Tennis Center, the 14-court municipal complex—10 indoor courts, 4 outdoor—is at Martin Luther King Way S and Walker Street. Play is for an hour and 15 minutes, for a fee; reservations are required— call (206) 324-2980.

North of downtown are 10 lighted outdoor courts at Lower Woodland Park, just off West Green Lake Way. Farther north, next to Nathan Hale High School at 30th Avenue NE and 107th, Meadowbrook has 6 lighted outdoor courts.

The Seattle Park Department has two other sizable clusters of courts. In West Seattle, across Fauntleroy Avenue from the northeast corner of Lincoln Park, are 6 lighted courts, all outdoors. At Magnuson Park, on Sandpoint Way NE and 65th NE are 6 unlighted outdoor courts.

For detailed information on reservations and about other courts throughout the city, call (206) 625-2168.

The city of Bellevue's park department operates an eight-court tennis center called Robinswood at 2400 151st Place SE. Four courts are covered and four are outdoors. The center is open seven days a week. During the winter, play is by the hour for a fee, with reservations required. The program includes lessons, group use, and tournaments. (Finding Robinswood is a job for a Sherpa. The best bet is to call (206) 455-7690 for reservations and road instructions.)

Six courts are located near Seattle-Tacoma International Airport, on South 188th Street near I-5—three on a high school campus and three in an adjacent county park.

Much of Seattle's tennis is played at private clubs. U.S.T.A. members with reciprocal privileges have seven choices, all listed in local telephone books.

Golf

Seattle has far more golfers than its courses can handle. To get in regular rounds, locals range as far north as Everett and as far south as Tacoma. Still, vacationers who can get out on weekdays can find starting times without undue trouble.

In town are three good municipal courses. Nearby are other courses open to public play.

U.S.G.A. members with reciprocal privileges will also find excellent courses among the private clubs in and around Seattle and the East Side.

In town. Jefferson Municipal (18 holes; 6,056 yards; par 70) is on Beacon Avenue south of downtown. Thick trees on a round-backed ridge make the course play longer than the card. West Seattle Municipal (18 holes; 6,054 yards; par 71) is just off Fauntleroy Avenue, the district's main stem. Brushy ravines and rolling terrain make life miserable for hackers. Jackson Park Municipal (18 holes; 6,070 yards; par 71) is just east of I-5 at exit 174, near the north boundary of the city. Thick stands of conifers make this rolling layout the tightest test of the three municipals.

South of town. Four courses come fairly close together. Earlington (18 holes; 5,218 yards; par 69) is a flat course in bottomlands on the opposite side of I-405 from Longacres Race Track. Foster (18 holes; 5,388 yards; par 68) is another low-lying course, but all wrapped up in a curve of the Duwamish River. It is on Interurban Avenue just south of I-5 Exit 156. Maplewood (18 holes; 5,625 yards; par 68) tucks away south of Renton on the Maple Valley Highway. It is hilly in front, flat in back. Tyee Valley (18 holes; 6,100 yards; par 71) is just off old U.S. 99 on South 192nd Avenue, 4 blocks south of Sea-Tac airport. The course rolls through stands of mature trees. It takes real concentration to putt in the shadow of a descending 747.

North of town. Here the roster is short; so are the courses. Brookside (9 holes, 18 tees; 5,800 yards; par 71) is east of Woodinville on NE 156th Street. Wellington Hills (9 holes; 2,735 yards; par 34) is close by State 522, the route from Bothell to Monroe. Wayne (18 holes; 4,812 yards; par 65) flanks Bothell Way at the south city limits of Bothell. The course is physically taxing because of its steep hills and the relentless presence of Sammamish Slough at the bottom of all those hills.

East of town. Bellevue Municipal (18 holes; 5,800 yards; par 70), on 140th Avenue NE, well north of the main shopping district, rolls gently through mature trees. Crossroads Golf Course (9 holes; 753 yards; par 3) is a gentle, open layout due east of 156th Avenue NE in Crossroads Park. Call (206) 455-6855 for directions. A privately owned driving range near Crossroads Golf Course rounds out the list of public golfing facilities close to the city of Bellevue.

These courses are about as far from downtown Seattle as most visitors to the city would care to go for a casual round. Collectors of golf courses can look slightly farther afield with real profit. The Snoqualmie-North Bend area, on I-90, has some fine courses (Snoqualmie Falls, Tallchief, and three others). Snohomish, on the Stevens Pass Highway, has two of the most challenging layouts in the region (Kenwanda and Snohomish).

Boating

Seattle has as good a claim as anyplace to the title of pleasure boating capital of the world. Its 40 miles of Puget Sound shoreline and 100 miles of lakefront are rife with marinas and private docks, most of them booked to capacity.

For just looking, the huge marina at Shilshole Bay in the Ballard district offers the most convincing panorama. The next largest complex is at Des Moines, a suburb south of the city.

Bustling with boats and brimming with nautical enterprises, Lake Union offers a striking counterpoint to downtown skyscrapers only a mile or two away. Among its attractions is the three-masted 1897 schooner *Wawona*, a 136-footer designed to carry huge cargoes with a small crew. At the Center for Wooden Boats, you'll find a replica of a Victorian boat-building shop and an outdoor museum of classic small craft, most rentable.

Visitors with their own craft can launch at dozens of public ramps, either on Puget Sound or Lake Washington.

For those who come without, rentals can be had in all sizes and styles.

Canoes and rowboats can be rented at Green Lake (next to Evans Pool on East Green Lake Way) for leisurely paddling and rowing on that small surface, or at the University of Washington Canoe House (just behind the football stadium) for more ambitious exploring in the channels to the north or the marshy lagoons across the mouth of the ship canal.

Along the Puget Sound shore, marinas offer sailboats for rent. Water skiers looking for powerful runabouts can rent them along Lake Washington.

Fishermen, who have less need for speed, can rent saltwater outboards in various locations (check the Yellow Pages under Boat Renting and Leasing).

Fishing

Washington State's famous fishing waters lie well away from Seattle, but the city has some reasonably productive areas, both fresh and salt water, right at its doorstep.

Elliott Bay, the water directly off the waterfront, is a fair source of blackmouth salmon (immature chinooks up to 20 pounds) during the winter months. It takes a hardy soul to venture out in the dawn light of a chill, ofttimes rainy day in an open outboard.

Ballard's Shilshole Bay has some salmon in its offshore waters.

More casual anglers can work for perch, flounder, and other smaller fry from the Shilshole breakwater, from Pier 57 on the downtown waterfront, from sea walls along Alki Drive in West Seattle, and from the sea wall in Ed Munro Seahurst Park in Burien.

Lake Washington supports bass, catfish, perch, and kokanee (landlocked sockeye salmon). The bass tend to be plentiful along the marshy shore of the University of Washington Arboretum as early as March. They also can be caught from public fishing piers in parks from Seward Park north to the Evergreen Point Floating Bridge. Kokanee, running to half a pound, also begin to be active as early as March. The other species come a little later.

The lake is open the year around for elusive trout (mostly cutthroat and rainbow).

The key to fine boating
Chittenden Locks connect Lake Washington with Puget Sound for 2,000 boaters on any warm weekend.

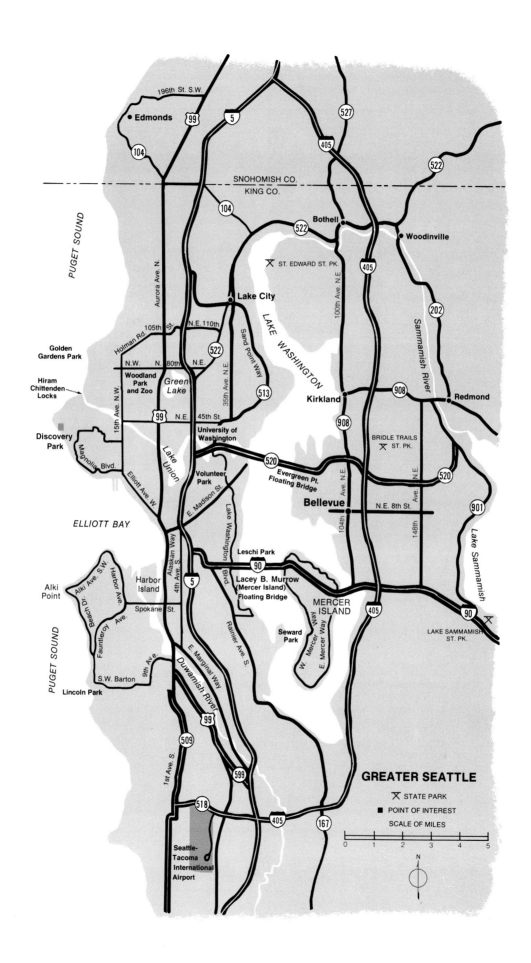

196th St. S.W.

● Edmonds

99

5

527

104

405

522

SNOHOMISH CO.
KING CO.

PUGET SOUND

104

522

Bothell ●

● Woodinville

✕ ST. EDWARD ST. PK.

405

100th Ave. N.E.

Lake City ●

LAKE WASHINGTON

Sammamish River

202

105th St.

N.E. 110th

Holman Rd.

Aurora Ave. N.

522

Sand Point Way

Golden
Gardens Park

N.W. N. 80th N.E.

513

908

Redmond ●

Hiram
Chittenden
Locks

Woodland
Park and Zoo

*Green
Lake*

35th Ave. N.E.

Kirkland

908

15th Ave. N.W.

99 N.E. 45th St.

BRIDLE TRAILS
✕ ST. PK.

Discovery
Park

Magnolia Blvd.

University of
Washington

520

901

Elliott Ave. W.

*Lake
Union*

Volunteer
Park

520

Evergreen Pt.
Floating Bridge

N.E. Ave. N.E.

148th Ave. N.E.

520

ELLIOTT BAY

E. Madison St.

Lake Washington Blvd.

Bellevue ●

N.E. 8th St.

104th Ave.

Lake Sammamish

Alaskan Way

4th Ave. S.

Leschi Park

90

Alki Ave. S.W.

Harbor Ave.

Beach Dr.

Harbor
Island

Lacey B. Murrow
(Mercer Island)
Floating Bridge

MERCER
ISLAND

405

90

Alki
Point

Spokane St.

Rainier Ave. S.

W. Mercer Way

E. Mercer Way

LAKE SAMMAMISH
ST. PK.

✕

Fauntleroy Ave.

9th Ave.

Seward
Park

5

PUGET SOUND

S.W. Barton

E. Marginal Way

Duwamish River

Lincoln Park

99

509

599

518

Seattle-
Tacoma
International
Airport

405

167

GREATER SEATTLE

✕ STATE PARK

■ POINT OF INTEREST

SCALE OF MILES

0 1 2 3 4 5

1st Ave. S.

N

Wineries and Microbreweries

Whether your taste runs to vintage Cabernet or freshly brewed ale, you'll find opportunities for touring and tasting at wineries and specialty microbreweries (breweries that produce less than 10,000 barrels annually) around the state.

Most of the wines are widely available. The specialty beers, however, are primarily sold on draft, and demand often exceeds the supply. Most taste best served close to home, when they're freshest.

Wineries. For decades Washington nurtured a slowly developing grape-growing and wine-making industry. Now that the plantings of European varietal vines have matured, the state has become a recognized leader in premium wine making. More than 50 wineries, many producing top-quality wines, are in operation. In international tastings, northwest wines repeatedly vie for top honors.

The state boasts three official wine-growing appellations, or specific combinations of climatic and geographic factors: the Columbia, Yakima, and Walla Walla valleys. All three regions receive only 8 to 10 inches of rainfall annually. Their northerly latitude, the same as France's Burgundy and Bordeaux regions, means ample hours of critical sunlight during the growing season.

White wine grapes grown in the eastern part of the state include Chardonnay, Sauvignon Blanc, Semillon, Chenin Blanc, Riesling, and Gewürztraminer. Among the reds are Cabernet Sauvignon, Merlot, Pinot Noir, Lemberger, and Grenache. Varieties grown in the western region tend to be cooler-climate grapes: Pinot Noir, Madeline Angevine, Muller Thurgau, and Riesling.

Almost all the wineries in the state welcome visitors. Many offers tours, but call ahead for specific times and directions to the winery. The largest winery in western Washington is Chateau Ste. Michelle in Woodinville, northeast of Seattle. The region east of the Cascades around Yakima and the Tri-Cities has the greatest number. Near the Tri-Cities, both Ste. Michelle's River Ridge Winery in Paterson and Preston Wine Cellars in Pasco offer comprehensive tours. In Spokane, Arbor Crest has a tasting room in an historic house; visits are by appointment only.

For an informative color brochure about Washington wines, along with a map of the wineries and their phone numbers and addresses, write to the Wine Marketing Program, 406 General Administration Building, Olympia, WA 98504. A pamphlet outlining a winery tour is available from the Tri-Cities Visitor & Convention Bureau, P.O. Box 2241, Tri-Cities, WA 99302. Another source of information is the Washington Wine Institute, 1932 First Ave., Room 510, Seattle, WA 98101. Several books discussing the region's wineries are available in bookstores, gourmet shops, and at some wineries.

Microbreweries. Since hops, one of the critical ingredients in beer, are grown in Washington in quantity, it's only natural that the brewing of premium beers should thrive. Rainier and Olympia, two large nationally known breweries, have been operating in Seattle and Tumwater, respectively, for decades. Both offer tours and tastings.

The boom in specialty beers is more recent, dating from 1982 when two microbreweries introduced their ales. Since that time four more companies have begun producing "craft beer." According to the beer-makers themselves, locally grown barley, excellent water, and the residents' increasing acquaintance with the specialty beers of Europe account for their growing popularity.

All the microbreweries produce ale, which tends to be complex, rich, and fruity, in contrast to the lighter, crisper lagers produced by large breweries. Other products include dark, rich stout, traditional porter, and ales made from wheat. Several of the breweries also produce seasonal (usually Christmas) variations.

Brewery taps and brewpubs sell beer on brewery premises. Some offer types not available elsewhere. A number of restaurants, pubs, and taverns offer a full selection of craft beers.

A few of the microbreweries have regularly scheduled tours; others welcome visitors only at certain times. Be sure to call ahead. The microbreweries are Hale's Ales, Colville (north of Spokane), (509) 684-6503, and Kirkland; Hart Brewing Company, Kalama (south of Longview), (206) 673-2962; Kemper Brewing Company, Poulsbo, (206) 697-1446; Kufnerbrau, Monroe (northeast of Seattle), (206) 784-4186; Red Hook Brewery (Independent Ale Brewery), Ballard (Seattle), (206) 784-0800; and Yakima Brewing and Malting Company, Yakima, (509) 575-1900.

Parks to taste

Seattle's array of city parks ranges from wide open spaces to urbane pockets. Green Lake (above) is one sort, home to child anglers, ducks, joggers, and eight-oared crews. An entirely different approach is Gasworks (right), where scrubbed-up machinery is an almost infinite monkey jungle for kids. Both are north of downtown.

Bellevue and the East Side

Originally bedroom communities for commuters into Seattle's downtown, Bellevue, Kirkland, Redmond, and the other communities on the east side of Lake Washington now boast offices of their own. Bellevue, in fact, is the fourth largest city in the state, with its own symphony and an art museum—atop the extensive Bellevue Square mall. During the summer, the city's Pacific Northwest Arts and Crafts Fair attracts above-the-norm craftspeople.

People get back and forth across Lake Washington, for the most part, via the Evergreen Point Floating Bridge, which connects with I-5 near the University of Washington and with I-405 just south of Kirkland. The more southerly Lacey V. Murrow Floating Bridge crosses Mercer Island as part of I-90; its link with I-405 is well south of Kirkland. Northwesterners have long since grown used to bridges that float on the water rather than soar high above it. The system is simple—concrete pontoons with air chambers—and durable.

Kelsey Creek Farm and Park, one of Bellevue's most popular parks, is located in the Richards Valley at 13204 SE 8th Place. This 30-acre farm includes farm animals, trails, an Oriental garden, a wildlife habitat, jogging trails, pastures, and a play area for children. The farm animals can be visited from 8 A.M. to 4 P.M., seven days a week; pony rides are available in the summer. For information regarding programs (and directions!), call (206) 455-6885.

Marymoor County Park touches the north end of Lake Sammamish near the town of Redmond. Among its facilities are tennis courts, a model airplane area, soccer fields, softball fields, an interpretive trail, a windmill, and more. A 1904 mansion to visit and a velodrome in which bicycle racers speed by are two of its attractions. When no scheduled competitions or other events are in progress, all comers can get onto the track and enjoy its 25° banked turns. The Sammamish River Trail follows the west shore of Lake Sammamish from Marymoor to Lake Sammamish State Park, near the south end of the lake. Walkers, joggers and bicyclists can then connect to the Burke Gilman Trail (page 25); equestrians can ride between Marymoor and North Creek. To reach the park from Seattle, take State 520 east to the West Lake Sammamish Parkway NE exit, State 901, and go south about ¼ mile.

Lake Sammamish State Park. Sprawling picnic lawns and a fine swimming beach have made this unit of over 400 acres one of the most heavily used of the region's summer parks. There is a boat launch for those who would fish the lake, water-ski, or otherwise get away from the beachbound throngs.

Waterfront Park in Kirkland, an extensive lakefront park, includes swimming beaches, fishing piers, picnic sites, and expansive lawns. Central Way leads from the I-405 exit marked Kirkland directly to it.

A short distance north of the shoreline, at 620 Market Street, an 1891 building houses a gallery, open Tuesday through Saturday.

Saint Edward State Park near Kenmore is the largest remaining undeveloped area on Lake Washington. Located on the grounds of a former seminary, its five miles of trail lead through forest to low-bank shoreline. To reach the park from I-405, go west on NE 116th Street to Juanita Drive NE, then north to the entrance.

Issaquah, east of Seattle, on I-90, boasts a skyport right beside the highway where spectators can watch parachutists and gliders. Gilman Village, a cluster of restored 19th-century buildings, houses shops and restaurants. Hiking trails lace the slopes of Squak and Tiger mountains, known locally as the Issaquah Alps.

Useful Addresses in Seattle

- Seattle–King County
  Visitors Bureau
  1815 Seventh Ave.
  Seattle, WA 98101

- King County–East Visitors Bureau
  1111-110th Ave., NE, Bldg. 100
  Bellevue, WA 98004

- Metro Transit Customer Assistance
  821 Second Ave.
  Seattle, WA 98104

- King County Dept. of Planning
  & Community Development
  Parks Division
  W226 King County Courthouse
  516 Third Ave.
  Seattle, WA 98104

- Seattle Parks & Recreation
  5201 Green Lake Way N.
  Seattle, WA 98103

- Bellevue Dept. of Parks & Recreation
  P.O. Box 1768
  Bellevue, WA 98009

- For addresses of music, theater, and sports organizations, see pages 21 and 23.

Logging towns, fishing
villages, and islands in
the sun give quiet pleasure

Outside Seattle, to both north and south, the Puget Sound basin holds a diversity of easy, friendly things to do.

This is Washington State's closest approach to a conurbation—a nose-to-tail string of cities. Tacoma almost runs into Seattle from the south; a long chain of suburbs reaches north from Seattle to Everett. And yet an old-time flavor still pervades this region. It grew up on fishing, farming, and logging. Though shipping, petroleum refining, and aircraft manufacturing are important industries today, the original occupations continue to play major roles.

A variety of islands gives Puget Sound much of its particular charm. The San Juans are the most numerous as well as most famous, but they are far from the only offshore retreats from a madding mainland. Enough islands separate themselves from the mainland by narrow, bridgeable gaps to give broad choice even to the boatless. The extensive Washington State ferry system brings several islands within reach of all; many more can be reached only by boat.

With literally 1,000 miles of Puget Sound shoreline, saltwater boating and fishing naturally lead the list of recreational pursuits. Their allies—clamming, tide pooling, and drift hunting—follow closely. In addition there are fine stream fishing for steelhead and trout, good watching for bald eagles and other birds, and a surprising amount of year-round hiking and bicycling.

The cities of Tacoma and Bellingham in particular have merit for the urbanite, and some quaint sound-side towns deserve exploration.

Weather. With minor variations, the climate patterns parallel those of Seattle. July and August are reliably dry and sunny. October through March is a period of frequent rain and even more frequent clouds. Spring and fall vary not only from day to day, but also hour to hour.

Temperatures hover within a narrow, mild range. In a typical year, a shoreside station records only three maximum temperatures in the 90s.

Rainfall varies more than temperature because of rain shadow effects from the Olympics.

Very little of the precipitation comes as snow at sea level, though the rare exceptions cause some wonderful traffic tie-ups. A mere 300 feet of elevation is enough to change a good deal of January and February precipitation to snow.

Highways. Interstate 5 cuts a wide, straight swath north and south. All freeway exits are numbered to correspond as closely as possible to mileposts. The numbers increase from south to north.

Those who will accept a turtle's pace as the price for great scenery can detour on two loops west of I-5. One byroad runs the length of Whidbey Island and part of Fidalgo Island, requiring a ferry ride at the south end. The other—State Highway 11, Chuckanut Drive—runs along a high bluff south of Bellingham.

Tacoma and Environs

To the south of Seattle, the Tacoma area is a pleasing extension of that curious mixture of urban, rural, and wild that characterizes the whole Puget Sound region.

The City of Tacoma

A mill town, deep-water port, neighbor to Fort Lewis and McChord Air Force Base, gateway to Mt. Rainier on one side and the Olympic Peninsula on the other, Tacoma reaches north to touch the Seattle metropolitan area and stretches south almost to Olympia. The Narrows Bridge connects it to the Kitsap Peninsula.

Accommodations. Tacoma has several large motels and hotels, many of them near I-5.

Attractions. When you drive I-5 through Tacoma, it's almost impossible to miss the massive Tacoma Dome, the scene of sports events, concerts, and trade shows.

Tacoma's old city hall, modeled after Renaissance hill castles in Italy, has been remodeled into

See additional maps on pages 34 and 37.

Sound

a collection of shops and restaurants. Aside from the shops and some excellent interior design details, what makes this restoration notable is its lofty clock tower, open to the public on weekends. Free guided tours to the 2½-ton clockworks begin hourly on weekend afternoons from Daley's Jewelry on the fourth floor. The building is at South Seventh and Commerce streets.

Nearby, specialty shopping and local events make the Broadway Plaza, between South 11th and South 13th streets, another focal point of the downtown. Two gleaming highrises—a hotel and a financial center—tower above a number of refurbished early-century buildings.

Still within a short distance are the Tacoma Art Museum, at South 12th Street and Pacific Avenue, telephone (206) 272-4258, and the Washington State Historical Society, at 315 North Stadium Way, telephone (206) 593-2830.

Parks and recreation. Well north of the downtown area, Point Defiance Park occupies a big part of the peninsula between the Narrows and Commencement Bay. Within the park are Never Never Land (storybook scenes), Fort Nisqually (a reconstructed Hudson's Bay Company trading post and museum), Forest Industries Museum (an outdoor replica of an old-time logging camp and a steam-powered train to ride on), a zoo (with well-selected, well-presented animals), and an aquarium (known for its octopi). The park also contains swimming beaches, rental boats and fishing gear, play equipment, picnic sites, rose gardens, and some excellent wooded walking trails. The ferry dock serving southern Vashon Island is on one edge of the park.

Between downtown Tacoma and Point Defiance, the Ruston Way waterfront has been revived with pocket parks, a walk-jog-bike trail with exercise stations, and new waterside restaurants. A spacious public fishing pier offers a fish-cleaning station, night lighting, a bait shop, and a snack bar. To reach Ruston Way, leave I-5 at City Center exit 133 and head north and northwest.

Plant lovers may wish to visit the botanical conservatory in Wright Park, close to downtown at South Sixth and South G streets. Orchids and other tropicals make up the principal permanent collection.

Across Commencement Bay from Point Defiance, Dash Point State Park has a swimming beach, some agreeable picnic grounds, and 138 campsites (28 hookups). It is most easily reached via State 509, an extension of South 11th Street from downtown. Tacomans support a diverse collection of public golf courses in and near town.

Outside the City

The mix becomes less urban and more rural and wild outside the city limits. East, south, and west of Tacoma is a miscellany of attractions.

Vashon Island has few formal parks. However, quiet roads through forest and along shore make it most agreeable for Sunday drives or bicycle excursions. For longer stays, bed and breakfast inns are available. Shops feature island-made edibles and crafts.

A ferry from Tacoma's Point Defiance docks at Tahlequah, on the south end of the island. Another ferry runs from the north end of Vashon to West Seattle and to Southworth on the Kitsap Peninsula. On the island, stub roads lead to quiet beaches, most of them on the west side. On the west side of Maury Island (actually a peninsula of Vashon), Dockton Park has children's play equipment, picnic tables, and stoves. A boat launch and boat moorage are found in Quartermaster Harbor.

Blake Island, off the northern tip of Vashon, is both a state park and home to a unique Northwest Indian attraction, Tillicum Village (see page 12). Park facilities include about 40 campsites, trails, and beaches.

The town of Steilacoom, on the Puget Sound shoreline, is a National Historic District. Maps for a self-guided tour are available at the Historical Museum at Lafayette and Main streets. The museum is open three afternoons each week; call (206) 588-8115. The Nathaniel Orr pioneer farmhouse and orchard are open April to October on Sunday afternoons.

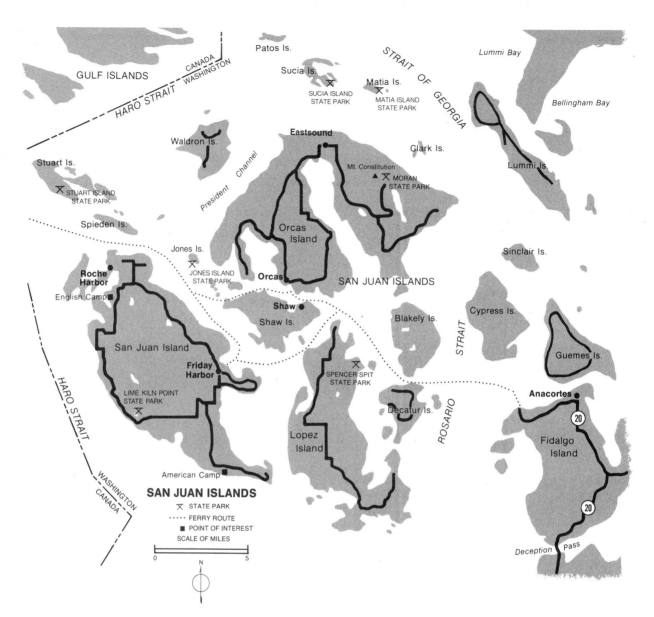

The ferry at the foot of Union Avenue leads to Anderson Island, which offers pleasant bicycling and beachcombing.

Near Steilacoom, the South Tacoma State Game Farm raises pheasant, steelhead, and rainbow trout. The grounds are also a refuge for local animals and migratory birds. Visitors may take a self-guided tour. To reach the farm, open daily, head west from I-5 at Exit 125, Bridgeport Way. At South 75th Street, signs mark the way.

South of Steilacoom on I-5, the Fort Lewis Military Museum explains military and Northwest history.

Puyallup. East of Tacoma, in the daffodil- and berry-farming town of Puyallup, the 17-room home of pioneer Ezra Meeker is open Wednesday through Sunday, 1 to 5 P.M. It is at 321 East Pioneer; telephone (206) 848-1770. Open during the same hours is the Western Frontier Museum of the Trails End Ranch at 2301 23rd Ave. SE; telephone (206) 845-4402. Puyallup is well known for the Puyallup Fair (actually the Western Washington Fair), held in September.

The Rhododendron Species Foundation adjoining the Weyerhaeuser offices in Federal Way, just north of Tacoma, offers acres of varied specimens of this remarkably diverse plant group. Most colorful in the spring, the gardens remain open all year. For more information, call (206) 927-6960.

Whidbey, Fidalgo, and Camano

These three large islands hug the eastern shore of Puget Sound so closely that bridges connect them

Water, water everywhere

Big, gentle ferries (below) are an imperative part of transportation on broad Puget Sound, as well as a stately pleasure. Sailboats (left) in a spanking breeze are an elective part of outdoor recreation. The choice rests between those who favor steady decks underfoot and those who walk a slant with joy.

to the mainland or to each other at three points. A ferry serves as the link at one spot. (Other ferries tie them to the San Juan Islands, Vancouver Island, and the Olympic Peninsula.)

Though less isolated than the San Juans, all three islands are quite rural, with a sprinkling of quaint towns. They are touched by "progress" only at the towns of Anacortes and Oak Harbor.

Whidbey Island

Most of Whidbey, Puget Sound's largest island, is peaceful and agricultural. It has fine state parks—each of distinct character—more of Puget Sound's shoreside towns, and several pokeabout roads.

At the south end, access is by ferry from Mukilteo on the mainland just south of Everett (Exit 189 from I-5). State 20 runs off the north end, across Fidalgo Island, and rejoins I-5.

From Clinton, the ferry terminus at the island's south end, it's a six-mile drive to Langley—three miles northeast of State 525 at the Langley Road.

This charming seaside village's art galleries, restaurants, and small shops are housed behind 1890s storefronts.

South Whidbey State Park, on the west shore about 10 miles from the ferry pier at Clinton, is a camping park with a shoal beach for swimmers, divers, clammers, and shore fishermen. A stand of old-growth forest is open to walkers. A loop road branches off State 525 to the 340-acre park.

Not far north, the turnoff to the Keystone ferry terminal (with ferries to Port Townsend on the Olympic Peninsula) also leads to Fort Casey State Park. Fort Casey was once a coastal defense post. The park preserves the old concrete battery emplacements and four guns. Also on the post, Admiralty Head Lighthouse has been turned into an interpretive display. The rest of the 137-acre, 35-campsite park mixes woods, open meadows, a 2-mile swimming beach, and short hiking trails.

Coupeville, 3 miles north, has a new town along State 20; the quaint original community of mid-1800s buildings lies east, along the water.

Puget Sound Ferry Routes

Ferries of many sizes and shapes ply the sheltered waters of Puget Sound on crossings as short as 7 minutes, as long as 4 hours.

They are transportation, restful interlude, and unusual experience all rolled into one, a special treat for visitors from drier parts of the world.

Usually there's no problem getting aboard, but reservations are required on the Victoria Clipper catamaran to Victoria, B.C., and recommended during the summer months on the other ferries to Canada.

Washington State Ferries, one of several ferry operators, handles most of the routes. For current information on most ferry schedules and fares, write Washington State Ferries, Colman Dock, Seattle, WA 98104. Telephone in Seattle: (206) 464-6400; statewide: 1-800-542-7052. Phone numbers for other ferry operators include Black Ball Transport, Inc., (206) 622-2222; B.C. Steamship, (206) 441-5560; and Victoria Clipper, (206) 443-2567.

The routes correspond to letters on the Puget Sound map.

Washington State ferries

[A] Anacortes–San Juan Islands–Sidney, B.C. (Vancouver Island); up to 3 hours, depending on number of stops (Lopez, Shaw, Orcas, San Juan/Friday Harbor).

[B] Mukilteo–Clinton (Whidbey Island); 15 minutes.

[C] Edmonds–Kingston; 25 minutes.

[D] Seattle (Pier 52)–Winslow (Bainbridge Island); 25 minutes.

[E] Seattle (Pier 52)–Bremerton; 60 minutes by car ferry; 35 minutes by passenger ferry.

[F] Fauntleroy (West Seattle)–Vashon–Southworth; 30 minutes.

[G] Point Defiance (Tacoma)–Tahlequah; 15 minutes

[H] Port Townsend–Keystone; 35 minutes.

Other ferry routes

[I] Anacortes–Guemes (Skagit County); 7 minutes.

[J] Port Angeles–Victoria, B.C. (Black Ball Transport, Inc.); 1 hour 35 minutes.

[K] Steilacoom–Ketron Island–Anderson Island (Pierce County); 30 minutes.

[L] Gooseberry Point (Bellingham)–Lummi Island (Whatcom County); 10 minutes.

[M] Seattle (Pier 64)–Victoria, B.C. (B.C. Steamship); 4 hours, May–October only.

[M] Seattle (Pier 69)–Victoria, B.C. (Victoria Clipper); 2½ hours.

Ebey's Landing National Historical Reserve, a 17,000-acre scenic area, is interpreted at the Island County Historical Society Museum, 1/2 mile north of State 20 at Alexander and Coveland streets.

Further up-island along State 20, another coastal artillery installation, Fort Ebey, has been made into a state park. Because of a rain shadow, the fort is one of the few places in western Washington where cactus is found. A few miles of hiking trails wander through the forest and along the beach; bass attract fishermen. The park has about 50 campsites and numerous picnic sites.

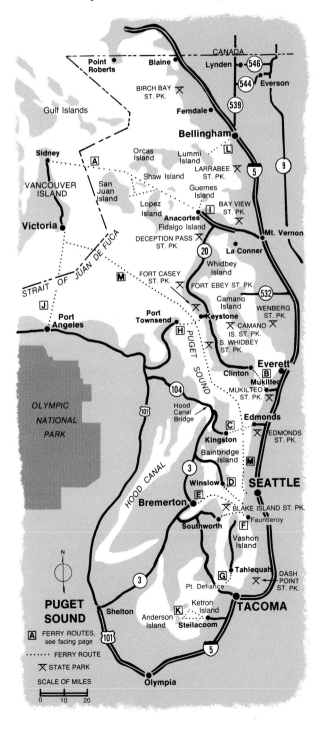

A dramatic stretch of turbulent water between islands, with a lofty bridge to look down from, is the main attraction at Deception Pass. About half of Deception Pass State Park occupies the northerly tip of Whidbey Island. The saltwater beach is mostly for strolling. A lake offers swimming areas, a food concession, and rental rowboats. Shady woods between the beach and the lake contain more than half of the park's 254 campsites.

On the east side of the highway is a boat launch, but most of this area is preserved untouched as the Cornet Bay Environments—a complex of salt water, fresh water, and forest. Hiking trails thread through the preserve.

Fidalgo Island

Fidalgo is most easily identifiable as the site of Anacortes, the gateway to the San Juans. It also holds the other half of Deception Pass State Park. The Fidalgo side of the park has a wooded waterside picnic ground at Rosario Beach and a boat launch, campground, and picnic area on Bowman Bay. Between these two areas is Rosario Head, with a fine view from its top and a fine undersea garden. Pass Lake is stocked with trout.

Anacortes, the major community on Fidalgo, is part fishing village, part oil refinery town, and, not least, the departure point for ferries to the San Juan Islands and Vancouver Island. In town is a museum with exhibits on local history; for hours and directions, call (206) 293-5198. Causland Park, three blocks west of the main street by way of Eighth Street, has unusual rock walls.

Major charter boat services operate at marinas on either side of Cap Sante, a tall rock at the northeastern corner of town.

The ferry terminal is well west of town. Further west, city-operated Washington Park has campsites, hookups, a long beach, and a boat launching ramp.

Similk Bay Golf Course (18 holes; 6,600 yards; par 72) is well groomed and plays as long as the yardage promises. It adjoins State 20, just on the island side of Swinomish Slough.

In addition to State 20, another bridge at La Conner gives access to the island some miles south. A county road runs from that lively village to connect with State 20 near Anacortes.

Camano Island

Camano echoes the long, looping profile of Whidbey Island, but in miniature. For years it has been a saltwater fisherman's retreat, with many private cottages, a few small shoreside resorts, and Camano Island State Park.

The park's 134 wooded acres shelter almost 100 campsites. Also at hand are covered cooking

Shoreside diversity

Man and Mother Nature share the long shore of Puget Sound in easy harmony. La Conner (above) typifies the picturesque fishing village of this region from waterfront to inevitable mountain—in this case Baker—peering over one shoulder. Where towns are not, beaches (right) beckon to picnickers, clammers, sometimes even to swimmers.

areas, a boat launching ramp, and moorages.

The island is easily accessible from Exit 212 off I-5, via State 530 and State 532.

The San Juan Islands

Clustered in upper Puget Sound are 192 islands—plus or minus a few, depending on the tide. These are the San Juans. A number are uninhabitable dots of rock. Most are thickly wooded, with fine beaches. Seventeen islands have boat-in state beach parks (Stuart, Sucia, Matia, and Jones are the most used), but only four islands are relatively developed, with towns, resorts, and campsites.

The accessible islands and the narrow waters between them are an inexhaustible source of recreation for boaters, especially those who care to fish (king and silver salmon, halibut, and rockfish), dig clams (rock cockles and softshells), explore tidepools, hunt drift, or picnic on unspoiled beaches. Swimming is chilly at best.

People without their own boats (rentals and charters are widely available) can use the San Juans, too. The state ferry system serves the four developed islands—Orcas, Lopez, Shaw, and San Juan—from Anacortes. The town of Friday Harbor on San Juan has an airstrip; scheduled service is available from several locations.

In addition to attracting the water-oriented, the main islands are a major destination for bicyclists. Private golf courses on San Juan, Orcas, and Lopez islands are open to visitors with reservations; greens fees are required.

Finally, resorts and bed and breakfast inns on these islands invite the urban weary to laze around. Night life is practically nonexistent.

San Juan Island. The economic and administrative center of San Juan County, this island offers rich natural and regional history.

Friday Harbor, site of the ferry terminal, is the largest community in the island group and anchor point for San Juan. At the top of the First Street hill, in one of the island's oldest buildings, the Whale Museum recounts the biology and behavior of these marine mammals. It's open daily in the summer; Wednesday through Monday the rest of the year. The San Juan Historical Museum is on Price Street, off Spring.

Whale and porpoise watching is the main attraction of Lime Kiln Point State Park, on the southwest side of the island. The lime kilns themselves, open to visitors, are just outside the park's boundary; the Lime Kiln Lighthouse is not open to the public.

One mile north of town, the University of Wash-ington research and teaching laboratory offers guided tours (on a limited basis) of its display tanks and aquarium; call (206) 378-2165.

Back in 1859, this island was the unlikely site of an unlikely war. San Juan Island National Historic Park commemorates the Pig War, so called because the only casualty was an English-owned porker shot by an American. This incident brought to a head the dispute between British and Americans over San Juan Island. Kaiser Wilhelm of Germany (of all people) mediated.

The national historic park comprises the campsites of the two rival garrisons. English Camp, 10 miles northwest of Friday Harbor, has four restored buildings and a restored formal garden, as well as a beach and picnic ground. American Camp, on the south side of Friday Harbor, also has beach and picnic grounds, as well as two restored buildings, an 1859 fortification, and a visitor center. The buildings are open in summer; the grounds are open daily all year.

Beyond American Camp, at the southeast tip of the island, is Cattle Point Natural Area—seven acres of sand dunes.

The town of Friday Harbor offers a number of accommodations, with others available in more isolated areas. San Juan County Park, about 15 miles from the ferry terminal along Roche Harbor and Marine View Drive, has some campsites in the main park and others for cyclists at some distance off the road.

Orcas Island. Largest of the four developed islands, Orcas has both a large number of resorts and a large camping park, Moran. One of the resorts (Rosario) is posh, with tennis courts and other refinements to go with a handsome old lodge.

Moran State Park, 13 miles from the ferry landing, has over 100 campsites, sheltered kitchens, picnic tables with stoves, hot showers, and other comforts. Almost 30 miles of hiking trails crisscross its nearly 5,000 acres. There is trout fishing in Cascade, Mountain, and Twin lakes. Cascade has rental rowboats and a swimming beach.

Within the park, Mount Constitution rises 2,400 feet above the surrounding sea, giving a 360° panorama of the islands, the Cascades, and the Olympic Mountains. A paved road to the top is popular with bicyclists.

In the village of Eastsound, the Orcas Island Historical Museum, housed in log cabins, exhibits Indian artifacts and pioneer relics. The museum is open afternoons from Monday through Saturday, Memorial Day to Labor Day. You can call for an appointment the rest of the year: (206) 376-4849 or 376-2316.

At Obstruction Pass, 80 acres of Department of Natural Resources land are open to the public.

Lopez Island. Flatter than the other islands, with half of its 50 miles of roads paved, Lopez is a particular favorite of easy-going bicyclists. The largest community, Lopez, has an historical museum.

Odlin County Park, a mile southwest of the ferry dock at Upright Head via Ferry Road, has a few campsites and a sandy beach. Spencer Spit State Park, 4.4 miles southwest of the ferry dock on Baker View Road, has both primitive and developed campsites and offers a protected lagoon for swimming. Hummel Lake has a camp for bicyclists, swimming, and some catchable trout.

Shaw Island. The ultimate escape among the islands served by ferries, Shaw has 17 miles of paved, hilly roads, one 6-unit county camping park at Indian Cove (2 miles southwest of the ferry landing), and no resorts at all. Franciscan nuns run the island's general store and the marina.

The Upper Puget Sound Shoreline

The mainland shore from Everett north offers highly attractive towns, resorts, and superb scenic drives.

Everett

Long a lumber port and mill town, Everett is now home to high-tech industry as well.

The Boeing assembly plant puts together pieces of 747s and 767s gathered from fabrication plants elsewhere around the United States. On weekdays, 90-minute tours (children must be twelve or older) show the giant planes in varying stages of production. The plant is at Paine Field, west of I-5 via Exit 189.

The same exit leads to the Mukilteo ferry pier, departure point for the boat to Clinton on Whidbey Island. The 1905 Mukilteo lighthouse is open on weekend afternoons.

In town, the marina offers visits to an historic schooner, the *Equator*, along with dining, shopping, and boat rental and excursions.

Migrating California sea lions claim the harbor's Jetty Island as their own from late winter to early spring; human visitors can take an excursion to see them. From July through September, when the sea lions are gone, free ferry service on Wednesdays through Sundays brings people to the island's sandy beaches.

The Everett Giants, a Class A affiliate of the San Francisco Giants, made Everett their home in 1983.

At Forest Park, west of I-5 exit 192 on Mukilteo

Boulevard, children can pet farm animals or ride ponies from May through September.

Kayak Point, on Marine Drive north of Everett, has 670 acres divided into a shoreline recreation area (boat launch, fishing pier, play area), overnight campsites, and a golf course.

La Conner and the Skagit Valley

Fields of bright tulips, irises, and daffodils make the Skagit Valley, some 75 miles north of Seattle between Mount Vernon and La Conner, a springtime delight. Maps of the flower fields are available at the Mount Vernon Chamber of Commerce (see page 42).

In the town of Mount Vernon, the Breazeale Interpretive Center, located at Padilla Bay on the Bayview-Edison Road, offers exhibits, a library, a nature trail, and an aquarium.

Old as a fishing village, new as a fun-junky source of arts, crafts, and antiques, La Conner is a collection of creaking piers, plain buildings, and fancy Victorians. It is home to bait shops, cafes, galleries, and boats. On summer weekends, excursion boats run along the slough and through other local waters.

A good bit of pioneer history lives on in La Conner. On First Street at Calhoun, Washington's oldest weekly paper, the *Puget Sound Mail*, still prints on the presses it started with in 1873. The imposing 3-story, 22-room Gaches Mansion at Second and Calhoun towers above the other local Victorian houses. For visiting hours, call (206) 466-4288. Nearby, the Volunteer Firemen Museum contains gear going back to the 1850s. On Fourth Street is the Skagit County Historical Museum.

Pioneer Park just south of town has playground equipment and picnic grounds.

Chuckanut Drive

For sustained scenery, no other road in the Puget Sound basin equals Chuckanut Drive (State 11). For more than 10 of its 20 miles, the road clings to a high bluff overlooking Rosario Strait and the San Juan Islands. Restaurants are sprinkled along the way, from Bow to Fairhaven.

The geographic midpoint and scenic high point, 1,884-acre Larrabee State Park runs from high hills down to the shore. At the shore is a boat launch. The rocky beach offers great tidepool looking at low tide; scuba divers enjoy these waters as well. Inland are some agreeable hiking trails and about 100 campsites (26 hookups).

At its south end, Chuckanut joins I-5 at Exit 231. At the north, it runs into the Fairhaven district of Bellingham. From there, drivers can enter town on city streets or slip onto 1-5 at Exit 250.

Bellingham

Bellingham faces Puget Sound with its wide-mouthed bay. Historic buildings and the influence of a university contribute to its appeal.

Accommodations. Despite its position in the narrow space between Seattle and Vancouver, B.C., Bellingham has many hotels and motels in or near town. The greatest concentration is south of the main business district and west of the freeway, on Samish Way between exits 252 and 253. Many bed and breakfast inns are available in Bellingham and Whatcom County.

Attractions. The city's waterfront is a working, industrial one for the most part. However, Harbor Center at Squalicum Harbor downtown offers shops, seafood restaurants, and a place to relax by the salt water. The busy marina here is the second largest on Puget Sound. During the summer, whale search cruises and San Juan Island cruises leave Bellingham's harbor regularly; charter boats are also available.

Housed in a splendidly ornate building, the Whatcom Museum of History and Art, at 121 Prospect Street, is free. It's open afternoons except Mondays; call (206) 676-6981. Inside, Bellingham's former city hall is both stately and attractive. The main floor is devoted to art, with Northwest painters dominating the permanent exhibits. The top floor has a small but lucid history of local logging, as well as an Indian display.

For more examples of vintage architecture, obtain a map for a walking tour of Victorian homes at the Roeder Home, 2600 Sunset Drive, or at the Whatcom County Park and Recreation Board Office, 3373 Mount Baker Highway.

Western Washington University's outdoor sculpture collection includes pieces by major American and British sculptors. A brochure describing a walking tour of the sculptures is available from the Visitors Information Center near the campus entrance. If you feel like more walking, a footpath leads from the campus up to 200-acre Sehome Hill Arboretum, which offers a native plant collection and a fine view.

Fairhaven, at the head of scenic Chuckanut Drive, acquired several ambitious brick buildings toward the end of the 19th century when locals thought it would become a major railroad terminal. The structures stood empty long after that dream died, but they are now home to a specialty shopping district.

Georgia-Pacific Corporation at 300 Laurel Street offers 1½-hour tours of the pulp- and paper-making process; telephone (206) 733-4410 for hours. No children under 12 are permitted.

Parks and recreation. Bellingham has developed some of the finest municipal parks in the region.

Both Boulevard Park (on the downtown waterfront) and Marine Park (in historic Fairhaven) are heavily used year-round for strolling, picnics, fishing, and kite flying. Spring through fall, they're good vantage points for watching early evening sailboat races.

At the Maritime Heritage Center, located downtown at 1600 C Street, you can learn about salmon any time of year and in the fall watch their tireless journey up the fish ladder. In season, you can also catch a steelhead or cutthroat trout to take home. For information, call (206) 676-6806.

Fairhaven Park, at the intersection of Chuckanut Drive with Hawthorn Road, features a large rose garden.

Cornwall Park, north of the downtown by way of Broadway and then Meridian, is a wooded oasis of calm within the city. Its spacious confines hold excellent picnic areas, children's play areas, and a long row of horseshoe pits.

Whatcom Falls Park, on the east side of town on Lakeway Avenue (Exit 252 from the freeway), offers the same range of activities plus a fishing pond for children and some pleasant short hikes along Whatcom Creek and Falls. Nearby, small Bloedel-Donovan Park, with a fine swimming beach, fronts on Lake Whatcom.

The largest (with 1,008 acres) and most diverse park is Lake Padden, which holds ball fields, a 3-mile trail around the lake, picnic sites, bank-fishing areas, two well-kept tennis courts, a swimming beach, and a municipal golf course. Lake Padden is accessible from I-5 via Samish Way, which passes by both the west and east gates of the park. Exits are 246 and 252.

At the south end of Lake Whatcom, Sudden Valley Golf Course (18 holes; 6,497 yards; par 72) allows some visitor play with reservations.

Between Bellingham and the Border

For travelers in a hurry, it's a quick trip from Bellingham to Canada—but those with time to explore the area will be richly rewarded.

Lummi Island, a quiet bit of country, is accessible via a 10-minute ferry ride from Gooseberry Point. To reach it from I-5, take exit 260 and head west on Slater and Haxton roads through the Lummi Indian Reservation. At the ferry landing are a seafood restaurant, a gift shop featuring Indian-made items, and a view of Hales Pass.

Lynden, also northeast of Bellingham, was settled by Dutch immigrants. The Pioneer Museum on Front Street is one of the largest museums of its kind in the state. Collections include over 40 buggies and other horse-drawn vehicles, Chevies from 1914 to 1931, old tractors and farm machinery, and Indian artifacts from the Queen Charlotte Islands.

The surrounding countryside offers dairy tours and U-pick berry fields.

Ferndale area parks. Three distinctive parks make Ferndale, on I-5 north of Bellingham, worth a stop. To get to the parks, take exit 262 (Axton Road), head west to the railroad underpass, and turn left on Neilson Road.

Hovander County Park preserves a typical family farm of this region. The house is open to tour; most of its rooms are furnished in livable fashion, while some are turned into display areas of memorabilia. The big red barn houses old farm equipment and a collection of animals that city kids can pet and get acquainted with. The remaining 60 acres contain hayfields, trails, fishing facilities, a treehouse and slide, picnic tables, and an overlook from the water tower.

At Tennant Lake, 200 acres adjoining Hovander Park, the Nielsen House has been adapted as an

---

Useful Addresses around Puget Sound

- San Juan Island
  National Historic Park
  P.O. Box 549
  Friday Harbor, WA 98250

Chambers of Commerce

- P.O. Box 340, Bellingham, WA 98227
- P.O. Box 1718, Blaine, WA 98230
- P.O. Box 1086, Everett, WA 98206
- P.O. Box 644, La Conner, WA 98257
- Lakewood, P.O. Box 99084, Tacoma, WA 98499
- 516 S. Second St., Mount Vernon, WA 98237
- Orcas Island, P.O. Box 252, Eastsound, WA 98245
- Puyallup Valley/Eastern Pierce County, 2823 East Main, Puyallup, WA 98372
- San Juan Island, P.O. Box 98, Friday Harbor, WA 98250
- Tacoma/Pierce County, P.O. Box 1933, Tacoma, WA 98401
- P.O. Box 304, Vashon, WA 98070
- North Whidbey Island, P.O. Box 883, Oak Harbor, WA 98227
- South Whidbey Island, P.O. Box 403, Langley, WA 98260

---

interpretive center. A half-mile system of trail and boardwalk, a bird-watching lookout tower, and a fragrance garden are all part of the park.

Pioneer Park, two blocks south of Main Street on First Avenue, features a collection of early log structures. Also on the 20-acre Nooksack River site are a pavilion and bandstand. Tours are available daily in summer; contact the Senior Center in the park for more information.

Birch Bay, on the coast just minutes from the Canadian border, has a roller arena, a water slide, a go-cart track, bicycle rentals, and a host of resorts with rough-hewn, immune-to-tracked-sand housekeeping cabins. Those whose tastes run away from aging cottages can find some modern motels, rentable condominiums, and commercial camping parks.

The bay floor is so flat that a modest tide goes out half a mile and a minus tide a mile or more, exposing a vast tract of clean, hard-packed sand and hundreds of shallow pools. The sand is good for digging horse clams (also called gapers) and cockles, great for sand castles, and eccentric as a softball field. The pools hold schools of tiny fish (mostly stickleback and baby flounder) and some legal-size Dungeness crab.

At high tide the shoals produce the warmest swimming water anywhere in the sound. Even moderately sunny days heat up the shallow waters.

Rangers at Birch Bay State Park, at the south end of the community, can explain much about the bay and its sea life. The park also has about 175 campsites (20 hookups) and some short walking trails through woods and alongside salt marshes.

Sea Links Golf Course (18 holes; 5,092 yards; par 68) lies right along the shore.

Peace Arch State Park is half in the United States, half in Canada. The big white arch spans the border, as do formal gardens, picnic areas, and children's play areas. The park adjoins the U.S. Customs station; use exit 276.

Semiahmoo, a spit reaching into Drayton Harbor west of Blaine, has both a resort and a county park. The resort features an 18-hole golf course designed by Arnold Palmer, a marina, and jogging trails. The day-use park offers boat rentals, an interpretive center, and restored cannery buildings. Horse, butter, and steamer clams can be dug on the beach. For directions, call (206) 332-4777. The area is also known for beachcombing and striking views of the mountains.

Light air to spare

The lofty Olympic Mountains shelter endless miles . . . but not all . . . of the sailor's paradise that is Puget Sound.

In this green world,
land and sea compete to
yield the richer rewards

The Olympic

It is hard to think of another place in North America where such mountains as the Olympics are so close to seawater on so many sides, with such dramatic results. On this smallish peninsula—75 miles north to south and 85 miles west to east—are the largest temperate-zone rain forests in the western hemisphere and an irrigated plain; storm-swept ocean waters and an inland sea so sheltered that people water-ski on much of it; ancient glaciers at 7,000-foot elevation and sea-level gardens that do not see frost from March until January.

So the Olympic Peninsula presents itself to visitors with astonishing generosity. The 1,431 square miles of Olympic National Park preserve the entire Olympic Mountain range and a 57-mile strip of coastline. The Olympic National Forest flanks the park all along its east and south sides and on its northwest corner, adding greatly to recreational opportunities. State and county parks amplify the choices still more, and private resorts take up where public lands leave off.

In sunny July and August, the peninsula looks—and is—paradisiacal. Its waters teem with fish (salmon, trout, halibut, cod) and shellfish (oysters, mussels, clams). Along roadsides, veritable cratefuls of wild berries hang waiting for pickers. Wildflowers abound—even the roadsides are lined with tall purple foxglove and sun-bright cone flowers.

The densely forested west side of the peninsula remains lightly populated. Even on the east side, with more arable land and far less rain, population scarcely presses on available space. People cluster at two places: the northeast portion of the peninsula, overlooking the Strait of Juan de Fuca and the entrance to Puget Sound; and along the southern stem, between the Pacific's Grays Harbor and southernmost Puget Sound.

Driving around the edge of the peninsula is an easy weekend's work. Indeed, "making the loop" on U.S. 101 is one of the rites of passage for Washingtonians. But once the numbing sense of awe wears off, recreation here can be a lengthy, even lifetime occupation for campers, high-country hikers, fresh and saltwater fishermen, oysterers, crabbers, boaters, naturalists, and collectors of panoramic scenery.

Weather. Exceptions in local weather patterns are so numerous that few rules are left to prove. The lofty barrier of the Olympic Mountains tears to shreds weather fronts coming in from the Pacific.

On the Pacific coast, most stations report annual average rainfall of more than 100 inches. At Quinault, the average is 134 inches; monthly totals break into double figures in October and stay there through March. In July and August, the averages are 2.6 and 2.8 inches. Snow is rare, as is summer heat.

On the east side of the peninsula, Bremerton receives 38 inches of rain a year, Port Angeles 24.6, Port Townsend only 18.3. Sequim, just 17 miles east of Port Angeles, gets a mere 16.8 inches of rain a year. In compensation for moderated rainfall, temperatures vary more widely than on the ocean side. Olympia has daily maximums in the 90° range on half a dozen days a year, and on rare occasion suffers at 100°. In winter, snow is rare near Puget Sound but likely in the foothills.

Up toward the tree line, the Olympic Mountains catch phenomenal volumes of precipitation. Rough estimates for the west side are the equivalent of 200 inches, which mostly falls as snow. Winter snow packs to a depth estimated at 500 inches. But nobody knows the precise figure.

Highways. One highway, U.S. 101, loops around the Olympic Peninsula, beginning at Aberdeen on Grays Harbor (see page 57) and ending at Olympia, at the southern tip of Puget Sound. On the west and north, a handful of stub roads lead away from the highway to beaches or mountains. On the east, Kitsap Peninsula adds a plentiful choice of roads, almost all of them two-laners. Most Olympic Peninsula roads are paved, though some of the stubs leading to extraordinary wilderness are graveled at best and muddy at worst.

Logging trucks and trailer or camper rigs are abundant. Traffic moves slowly.

Freeways are scarce in the region. The stretch of U.S. 101 between Olympia and Shelton, State 16/3 along the Kitsap Peninsula from Tacoma Narrows

See additional maps on pages 49 and 57.

Peninsula

Seattle   Spokane

up to Silverdale, and U.S. 12/State 8 across the base of the peninsula between Aberdeen and Olympia are the only ones.

The Sheltered East Side

The sheltered side of the Olympic Peninsula is the most human and diverse, offering every kind of salt and freshwater recreation, high mountains, and a sprinkling of colorful shoreside towns.

Two quite different ways to travel the territory present themselves. U.S. 101 along Hood Canal is direct and scenic, with a minimum of towns, maximum access to the mountains, and good exposure to tidewater. The other route, east of that, wanders through a maze of islands, peninsulas, and bays on the Kitsap Peninsula, providing many opportunities to explore beaches.

Hood Canal Shoreline along U.S. 101

The Hood Canal shoreline invites a dawdling exploration of a long series of excellent parks, an intertidal zone rich with clams and native oysters, and fine scenery.

Though Hoodsport is the only community between Shelton and Sequim large enough to be called a town, restaurants and motels appear often along the 75-mile route. And a resort complete with tennis courts, golf course, and moorage is on the canal just east of Union.

Shoreside parks begin where the highway joins the canal for northbound motorists.

Potlatch State Park is a small camping unit—35 sites, 18 hookups—but a major day use area. Mobs come at low tides to pick oysters, dig clams, and catch crabs at one of the richest public beaches.

Less than a mile north, Cushman Beach—the outflow from Tacoma Power Company's hydroelectric plant—also has oysters and clams.

The town of Hoodsport lies not far north of Cushman Beach. At the highwayside local cafe,

the less adventurous need climb only six steps to taste the best of local oysters. For boaters, the public dock has a boat moorage across the road. Hoodsport Winery is open daily for tours and tasting; call ahead to (206) 877-9894.

Some 4 miles north, Lilliwaup Recreational Tidelands offers more oyster and clam beds. There is not much announcement—just pullouts north of the low bridge across Lilliwaup Creek.

Neighboring Eagle Creek Recreational Tidelands adds crabs to the roster of edible quarry.

Beyond Eagle Creek comes a long dry spell for all save the locally knowledgeable. Pleasant Harbor State Park breaks the drought. The park is principally a boat moorage, but its short beach does have both clams and oysters. Dosewallips State Park, less than 2 miles north, is the principal park on the upper canal. Its 425 acres of meadows and woodlands straddle U.S. 101. Dosewallips has almost 150 campsites (40 hookups) and hiking trails to go with beaches on both sides of the Dosewallips River mouth. Clams, oysters, and crabs can all be found here.

Only a few hundred yards farther north is the U.S. Forest Service's Seal Rock Campground, with 14 tent camps and 20 trailer sites, 10 picnic sites, and a long beach with clams and oysters.

Mountain Side of U.S. 101

The North Fork of the Skokomish River above Lake Cushman is the great gateway into the high Olympics from their easterly side. Close by, the Hamma Hamma and Dosewallips River watersheds offer other routes into the mountains.

Both backpackers and fishermen use the country all summer; in winter are steelhead runs.

Staircase Campground is the National Park Service base point for both day hikers and high-country campers. In woods alongside a dramatic sequence of rapids on the North Fork of the Skokomish are 59 fine campsites.

A 5-mile nature walk loops around the river valley from the campsites. Other trails along the west side of the river offer fine day hikes.

Challenges in variety

On the Olympic Peninsula, the high country of the national park (above) has goats that think any lunch is theirs to share. (An introduced species, the goats are a serious resource problem to park management and a threat to visitors.) Down along the shore, man has mainly himself to contend with. Port Townsend (right), as its buildings demonstrate, burgeoned with San Francisco in the 1880s. It never became a major city but saved a good deal of peace, quiet, and Victorian architecture.

The confirmed high-country hiker will find this a prime access point to most of the park's 600 miles of trails and can travel cross-country to either the north or west entrances to the park or retrace steps to the starting point.

Staircase Road departs from U.S. 101 in downtown Hoodsport. A ranger is on duty during the summers.

Lake Cushman State Park is on Staircase Road 10 miles closer to Hoodsport. With 80 campsites (30 hookups) and two boat ramps, the 565-acre park caters to fishermen pursuing cutthroat trout. However, the isolated, woodsy site also is popular with hikers who prefer gentle foothills.

Another 22 lowland lakes in the region have public fishing access, mostly for trout but also for kokanee (sockeye salmon).

Some of these smaller lakes have Washington State Department of Natural Resources campgrounds on their shores.

Hamma Hamma Recreation Area, north of Hoodsport with access from U.S. 101, follows the Hamma Hamma River from lowlands through foothills and on into the high country of the national park. Most of the development was done by the U.S. Forest Service within the Olympic National Forest. National Forest Service campgrounds are Lena Creek (7 R.V., 7 tent sites) at 700 feet and the walk-in Lena Lake (10 tent sites) at 1,800 feet.

One of the most popular day hikes on all the peninsula is the Lena Lakes trail, connecting Lena Creek and Lena Lake campgrounds.

The Dosewallips River course has, in addition to Dosewallips State Park and Seal Rock Campground on Hood Canal, one foothill campground—Dosewallips Campground, with 33 tent sites.

The Dosewallips, Skokomish (the main stream, not the north fork), Satsop, and Duckabush are the most productive winter steelhead streams on the east side of the peninsula.

The district Forest Service ranger station at Hoodsport, a few yards off U.S. 101 on Staircase Road, has maps and trail information.

Shelton is 12 miles south of the Hood Canal. Many Christmas trees are harvested from tree farms near this town. The chamber of commerce, located in a caboose parked downtown, is a storehouse of published information on outdoor recreation in this part of the world.

South Sound state parks. East of Shelton via Pickering and Wingert roads, Jarrell Cove State Park on Hartstene Island is a popular spot for boaters. It offers 20 campsites and a day-use area with kitchen shelters. Four satellite parks—Squaxin Island, Stretch Point, Eagle Island, and McMicken—can be reached only by boat.

Penrose Point State Park, accessible via a local road heading south from State 302, is on Key Peninsula, which extends into the Sound between Shelton and Tacoma. A day-use area for clam digging, picnicking, and beachcombing, as well as a few miles of hiking trails, supplements the 83 campsites and 3 kitchen shelters. The park has 8 moorage buoys, a dock—and a petroglyph.

Kitsap Peninsula

Of all the untidy sculpture left over from the last ice age in the Pacific Northwest, the Kitsap Peninsula is least orderly. In truth it is hard to think of Kitsap as one peninsula, since it is an endless collection of bays and points bounded on one side by Hood Canal and on the other by the main body of Puget Sound. However, the whole collection anchors to the mass of the Olympic Peninsula near Shelton, and it really is one peninsula.

State 3 up Kitsap's spine serves as a diverting alternative to U.S. 101 for those Olympic Peninsula visitors whose taste runs more to picturesque small towns than to mountains. The peninsula can also be reached by ferry from Seattle or Edmonds, or by way of the Narrows Bridge from Tacoma.

Bremerton. A major U.S. Navy shipyard and the ferry terminal connecting with Seattle are located here. Any of several sizable motels near State 3 in the northwest portion of town can be a useful anchor point for visitors.

Within easy walking distance of the ferry terminal is a Naval Museum, located at 130 Washington Avenue next to the Bremerton/Kitsap County Visitor and Convention Bureau. Those wishing a close look at the big ships can ride the Bremerton–Port Orchard foot-passenger ferry from the First Street pier right past them.

Attractions along the peninsula. Alternating with dense stands of Douglas fir, towns and attractions reflect the diverse quality of life along Puget Sound.

Gig Harbor, at the base of the Kitsap Peninsula, began as a small harbor for fishermen. It is still that, but around the core has grown a tourist village of art and craft shops, shoreside restaurants, and pleasure-boat marinas. The town is just off State 16, 4 miles north of the Narrows Bridge from Tacoma or 21 miles south of Bremerton.

Silverdale, along State 3 about 8 miles north of Bremerton, has sprouted housing developments and a mall as a result of the growth of the Bangor Submarine Station. The town is also home to the Kitsap Historical Museum.

Poulsbo, roughly halfway between Bremerton and Port Gamble, is just off State 3 (on State 305, leading to Bainbridge Island). Until recently the town was an enclave of Norwegians, and its Norse heritage is still reflected in its shops, restaurants, and festivals. Poulsbo's Marine Science Center, 17771 Fjord Drive NE, offers educational exhibits and live saltwater denizens.

Further along State 305, the Suquamish Museum showcases the world of the region's original inhabitants. The museum is 40 minutes from downtown Seattle via the Winslow (Bainbridge Island) ferry. Other points of interest on the Port Madison Indian Reservation include Chief Seattle's grave, the site of Old Man House, a nature trail, and the Suquamish Fish Hatchery. For further information, call (206) 598-3311.

Winslow, 12 miles south of Poulsbo on State 305, is Bainbridge Island's cross-sound ferry connection to Seattle. A few choice shops and a winery open for tastings are among its attractions; the island also holds two state parks.

Port Gamble, 23 miles north of Bremerton via State 3, is a one-time lumber company town that has turned itself into a museumlike village. In the basement of the Port Gamble Market, the historical museum traces the logging industry in a region now harvesting its third crop of trees. It's open from Memorial Day through the first weekend in October. In the old general store on State 104, Of Sea and Shore Museum houses aquariums and a collection of shells and marine fossils from around the world.

The nearby Cyrus T. Walker Nursery and Forest Research Center provides a greenhouse tour and a film about growing trees.

Besides connecting directly to Bremerton by road, Port Gamble is 8 miles from the Kingston ferry terminal (connecting to Edmonds) and 1 mile from the Hood Canal Floating Bridge that leads onto the rest of the Olympic Peninsula.

Still farther north on a county road, the village of Hansville is near the tip of the Kitsap Peninsula. Camping resorts here rent open boats, motors, and gear for fishermen seeking salmon. Here also is Point No Point Lighthouse.

Waterside parks. State and county parks with every degree of development dot the shorelines of Kitsap Peninsula and the islands alongside it. Many of the beaches can be reached only by boat, but more than enough are accessible by car.

Twanoh, Belfair, Scenic Beach, and Kitsap Memorial state parks are on Hood Canal.

Twanoh, 25 miles west of Bremerton on State 106 (a connector to U.S. 101), is highly developed. It has nearly 400 campsites, 9 hookups, food and grocery concessions, tennis courts, a sandy beach, boat launch, and moorage.

At this point, Hood Canal angles east-west instead of north-south. Its waters are calm and shallow, fine for swimming and water-skiing.

Belfair State Park, on a stub road leading west from the town of Belfair, is much more rustic. Its pebbly shoal beach is a favorite with oyster pickers. The park has almost 200 campsites, 47 hookups, and abundant picnic tables; many are shaded by conifers, but some are open. The park sits at the inner tip of Hood Canal.

Scenic Beach State Park, west of Silverdale on a county road, has 50 campsites within its 88 acres. There are a boat launch and a good beach.

Northernmost of the state parks is Kitsap Memorial, a 58-acre, 43-campsite beach park with picnic facilities and a boat moorage (but no ramp). It's just south of the Hood Canal Bridge on State 3.

In addition to these state parks, the Kitsap side of Hood Canal has a county park and several public beaches maintained by the Washington Department of Natural Resources. Most of the DNR beaches are accessible only by boat.

On the Puget Sound side of the peninsula are four more beach parks.

Five miles west of Gig Harbor, Kopachuck State Park provides about 40 campsites, a day-use picnic area with shelters, moorage facilities, and an underwater scuba park. Just offshore, Cutts Island is a favorite stop for boaters. It is believed to have been an Indian burial ground, hence its other name—Deadman's Island.

Three miles northeast of Bremerton via State 306, Illahee State Park offers visitors a prime bit of Puget Sound waterfront, complete with view and pebbly beach. It has 25 campsites, picnic tables, and a boat launch.

Fay Bainbridge State Park, at the northern tip of Bainbridge Island, is accessible via the Winslow ferry from Seattle or by State 305 from Poulsbo. The 17-acre beach park has 30 campsites, a boat launch and moorage, and picnic sites. About 12 miles southwest is Fort Ward State Park, a day-use area on the site of a coastal fortification.

Port Townsend

The legacy of the town's early plans includes some fine Victorian architecture and three state parks—attractions that have drawn a community of artists and artisans.

The town sits at the tip of its own peninsula, due north of the Kitsap Peninsula; it faces east across Puget Sound toward Whidbey Island. It can be reached by ferry from Whidbey (Keystone), over the Hood Canal Floating Bridge from the Kitsap Peninsula, or by State 20 from U.S. 101.

A small business district runs along a narrow shelf next to the waterfront and includes a variety of art and craft shops, many in restored brick buildings.

In the spring and summer, festivals and cultural events abound.

Accommodations. Bed and breakfast accommodations flourish in Port Townsend's legacy of historic buildings. In addition, several comfortable motels are located on State 20 just west of the main business district. Modern resort condominiums are also available. One uncommon possibility is Manresa Castle, an elegantly restored mansion. Another unusual option is a duplex in the officers' row of Fort Worden State Park.

Attractions. The principal attractions in town are the historic buildings—and the galleries, antique shops, and restaurants they house.

A tour map with locations and background sketches of nearly 70 points of interest is available at the visitor center at the entrance to town;

telephone (206) 385-2722. The Starrett House on Clay Street and the Rothschild House at Franklin and Taylor are open for tours.

Jefferson County Historical Museum is in the old courthouse, a masterwork of architectural overstatement.

Parks and recreation. Port Townsend's ring of forts-turned-parks (Worden, Flagler, and Townsend) offers remarkably diverse recreation. Other facilities include boat anchorage just off the historic waterfront district and near-town marinas and launching ramps. Great salmon fishing is complemented by good clam, crab, and oyster beaches. The town has public tennis courts and golf courses.

Fort Worden State Park, immediately adjacent to town, now serves as a conference ground and

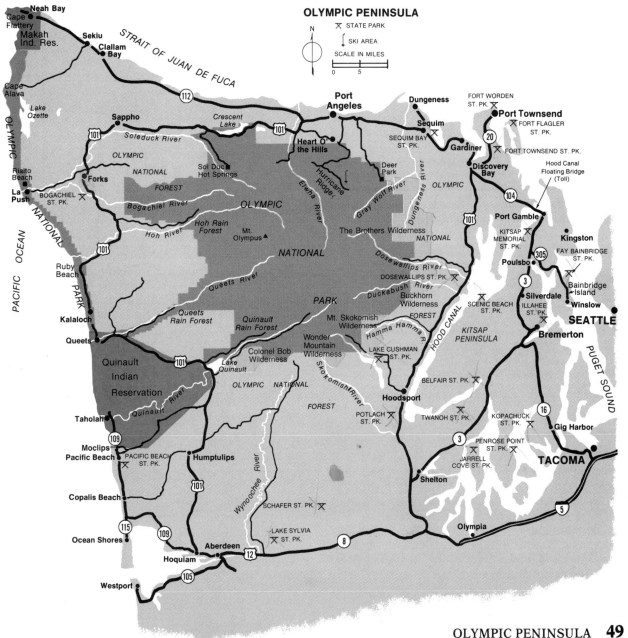

OLYMPIC PENINSULA

✕ STATE PARK

⛷ SKI AREA

SCALE IN MILES

0   5

art center as well as a park. Its beaches, lawns, and picnic sites are open to day use. Visitors can watch artists in residence and visit the restored and furnished commanding officer's house, a military museum, and a marine science center. Overnighters can use campsites or arrange for rooms in one of the refurbished officers' row houses; call (206) 385-4730.

Fort Flagler State Park, some miles south of town on State 20, then east on a county road, is the park for fishermen and outdoorsmen. Another former coastal artillery post, it now holds over 100 campsites, some hiking trails, and kitchens and picnic sites on its 783 acres. Beaches are its prime asset. The park has a boat launch for salmon fishing or pot fishing for crab; clams are available within the park and at four other nearby beach accesses. A concessionaire rents boats and sells fishing tackle and groceries.

Flagler sits on Marrowstone Island. Two narrow bays between it and the peninsula holding Port Townsend are rich in sea life. One of those bays is an underwater park and learning center.

Between Fort Flagler and Port Townsend, Old Fort Townsend State Park offers a spacious lawn and a serene stand of woods on a bluff looking east. Its beach has both clams and crabs. Secluded picnic sites round out the facilities for day visitors; a small group campground has 40 tent sites.

Port Ludlow, an old-time mill town 20 miles downsound from Port Townsend and 8 miles north of the Hood Canal Floating Bridge, has a resort with tennis courts, a fine golf course, rental boats, a 300-slip marina, and swimming.

The Strait Side

If Puget Sound is sheltered and civilized, and if the Pacific beaches are stormy and wild, then the Strait of Juan de Fuca on the north side of the Olympic Peninsula is a graceful bridge between the extremes.

Port Angeles

As a natural stopover point, Port Angeles has a substantial collection of motels, bed and breakfast inns, restaurants, and other services for visitors. It serves as gateway to shore and mountains—and to Victoria, B.C., a 1½-hour ferry ride away.

The National Park Service maintains a visitor center and historical museum at 3002 Mt. Angeles Road. It's a 17-mile drive along this road from Port Angeles to Hurricane Ridge.

Sequim-Dungeness

The folk of Sequim make much of the unlikely fact that local farms and gardens must be irrigated for lack of rainfall. The Olympics cast their strongest rain shadow across this small valley, leaving it with as few as 10 inches of precipitation a year, and seldom more than 18. This mild, dry weather has made the town a popular retirement haven, complete with parks and golf courses.

Accommodations. Though not plentiful, a few motels flank U.S. 101 in Sequim. Dungeness has cottage resorts along its bay front. There are several R.V. parks. At Sequim Bay is another resort and camper park.

Attractions. There are two wineries in Sequim, both open to tours and tasting, but call first: Neuharth is (206) 683-9652; Lost Mountain is (206) 683-5229.

The Olympic Game Farm between Sequim and Dungeness breeds Siberian tigers and other endangered species. The farm is also home to several four-footed movie stars when they are not working. From April through October, visitors may drive through the 180-acre preserve, watch the animals from the observation area, or join a guided walking tour.

A working oyster farm, open to visitors, nestles below the bluffs at Dungeness.

Parks and recreation. Sequim Bay State Park, on the bay east of town, has 86 campsites (26 hookups) in its 92 wooded, shoreside acres. There are sheltered picnic sites, a swimming beach complete with clams, a boat launch, and tennis courts.

Dungeness Recreation Area, a Clallam County park occupying the base of Dungeness Spit, has several picnic areas and 67 campsites in mixed scrub and woods. A walking trail through the Dungeness National Wildlife Refuge leads out onto sandy Dungeness Spit itself. Its seaward beach, 5½ miles long, is laden with driftwood. Shore fishing there is productive, and birds in variety can be seen. On the inner side, both clams and crabs can be caught by waders, though boats and pots make crabbing easier. A state park boat-launching ramp is at Cline Spit, accessible from the village of Dungeness.

Two challenging golf courses flank Sequim. Dungeness Golf Course (18 holes; 6,900 yards; par 72), north of U.S. 101 via Kitchen Road, is fairly open but persistently rolling and heavily trapped.

Pointblank mountains
From Hurricane Ridge in Olympic National Park, auto tourists get a close look at glaciated peaks.

On the road to Dungeness, SunLand (18 holes; 6,475 yards; par 72) is more level.

Finally, the floor of Dungeness Valley makes for easy bicycling on alternate roads north of U.S. 101. Maps of recommended routes are available at the Sequim visitor information office on U.S. 101.

The Salmon Ports

State 112 is a road for salmon and halibut fishermen. Beginning at Port Angeles and running almost to the northwest tip of the Olympic Peninsula, the route is dotted with towns and resorts catering to fishermen.

In addition to the Port Angeles marinas inside Ediz Hook, a camper park at Agate and Crescent beaches offers both charter and rental boats.

Clallam Bay and Sekiu lie close together some 50 miles west of Port Angeles. Half a dozen resorts and camper parks offer rental boats or charters.

Neah Bay, in the Makah Indian Reservation, is the farthest west and busiest of the sport-fishing towns. Large resorts operated by the Makah tribe offer both charters and boat launching. Where the road turns into town, the Makah Cultural and Research Center has handsome displays including a replica of a cedar longhouse, authentic dugout canoes, and archaeological artifacts.

The beaches at and near all these resorts are also popular sources of driftwood and agates.

Beaches near the town of Joyce, between Port Angeles and Clallam Bay, have smelt runs.

Inland from the Strait

Within a few miles of the beaches, the north side of the Olympic Peninsula offers a startling range of lowland lakes and towering alpine peaks. With them come fine fishing streams.

Heart O' The Hills–Hurricane Ridge. From Port Angeles, Hurricane Ridge Road runs south, begins its twisting climb before it gets to Heart O' The Hills Campground, then keeps on climbing up to Hurricane Ridge. The campground, with 105 sites, is one of the largest summer camping units in Olympic National Park as well as a launch point for hikes up to Hurricane Ridge.

Further up Hurricane Ridge Road is a day lodge (light meals only). From there, a 1½-mile nature trail leads to 5,757-foot Hurricane Hills. Clear-day views are spectacular: from glacier-crested mounts Carrie and Olympus, across the Strait of Juan de Fuca to Vancouver Island.

The unpaved ridge road brings hikers closer to alpine heights.

The Olympics offer little in the way of winter recreation. Sea-girt, they collect snow often too wet and heavy for good snowshoeing, cross-country skiing, or even snowmobiling. The lone exception is Hurricane Ridge, which is high enough to get drier snow and sheltered enough to keep the depths within reason. In winter the lodge becomes headquarters for a day-use ski area with 500 vertical feet of runs, one poma, and two rope tows. Ski rentals are available.

Elwha River. About 10 miles west of Port Angeles, Elwha Road slips south from U.S. 101 up the Elwha River drainage. Along its lower course, this waterway is one of the most productive steelhead streams on the peninsula. The National Park Service has a 41-site campground just below Lake Mills. Further up tributary Boulder Creek, along a washed-out road, is a walk-in campground with 20 tent sites. In addition to providing fishing access, the campgrounds are trailheads for high-country hikers. The Elwha is also a good choice for a raft trip.

Lake Crescent. Cradled among gentle hills more than mountains, long Lake Crescent is a tranquil haven in otherwise tumultuous country. Entirely within the national park boundary, the lake supports a diverse population of trout, which can be caught without a state license.

Concessionaire resorts at each end of the lake have launching ramps and rental boats. Lake Crescent Lodge on U.S. 101 is the largest resort on the lake. A national park visitor center at Storm King on U.S. 101 and several picnic grounds round out the facilities.

At the east end of Crescent is small, shallow Lake Sutherland, which is warm enough for swimming and yet cool enough for cutthroat trout.

From Fairholm at the west end of Crescent, a road (closed for repairs until 1988) runs alongside the Soleduck River. The road leads to a national park campground, a high-country trailhead, and a hot-spring resort.

The Peninsula's Ocean Side

From the peninsula's northwesternmost tip down to Ruby Beach, the Pacific shoreline is rocky, stormswept, and remote. Four roads lead out to the shore, but no road runs along it for a shade more than 50 miles. Here is the ultimate opportunity for hikers on wild beaches. Inland from this shore is quite an opposite world: deep rain forests that fill river valleys with a serene, often silent sort of wilderness. For about 15 miles northward from the mouth of Grays Harbor, civilization rules along broad, sandy beaches famous for their hordes of razor clams—and hordes of diggers.

Wild Beaches

Most of the wild beaches toward the northern tip of the peninsula are for hikers. At Rialto and La Push, however, stub roads come to the backshore; then at Kalaloch U.S. 101 sticks close to the beaches for several miles, opening up the region.

Cape Flattery and Shi-Shi Beach. Cape Flattery is wondrously rugged and hard to use even though it adjoins comfortable Neah Bay within the Makah Indian Reservation, some 66 miles west of Port Angeles. However, the makeshift road and the walk beyond it repay the effort in full. The steep wave-wracked cliffs and offshore rocks provide scenery unique in the region.

Shi-Shi Beach is reached by the next best thing to no road at all. The road, such as it is, branches away from the road to Cape Flattery not far west of Neah Bay. An abandoned school bus marks the end for all cars of normal manufacture. From there the hike wanders through scrub to a serene 3-mile crescent of sand between Portage Head and Point of the Arches. The latter, a dramatic array of wave-tunneled rocks, closes off any access to the south.

Cape Alava and Lake Ozette. The only access to the shore in the 30 miles of coast between road's end at Neah Bay and road's end at Rialto/La Push is by trail from Lake Ozette.

The lake itself is among the largest in the state. Though traces of logging remain along the east shore, Lake Ozette is now completely within Olympic National Park.

A resort with a campground is in the park at the northern tip of the lake, where the 22-mile road from Sekiu ends. From here, one trail wends out to Cape Alava; another goes out to Sand Point. The trails and the shore make a rough equilateral triangle, 3 miles to a leg. Hiking this is a fine introduction to the area. The hardy can do it in a day; most hikers camp or do only one leg.

Cape Alava, westernmost point in the 48 connected states, lies at the end of the more northerly trail, 3.3 miles from the resort. Partially a boardwalk, the trail is muddy but easy walking through moss-festooned forest carpeted with ferns, salal, bunchberry dogwood, and young trees sprouting from the remains of fallen giants. Small meadows change the pace. Surf is audible for a long time, but the Pacific remains hidden until a walker steps onto the beach.

This picturesque point is the site of an abandoned Indian village. A Washington State University archaeological dig, now closed and covered up, yielded artifacts that can be viewed at the Makah Museum in Neah Bay. From the point, hikers can head either south toward Sand Point or north toward an uncommon island and marine garden.

North a mile is Cannonball Island, named for large spherical concretions that wash out of its steep side. The island (also called Indian Island) lends itself to exploration at low tide, but getting trapped on it means sitting out a 12-hour tide.

About a mile north of the island, Carson Sea Cave forms an impressive garden of intertidal plants and animals. It can be explored only at low tide. Just beyond, the mouth of the Ozette River closes off any further push to the north.

Between Cannonball and Carson, hikers may come across bits and pieces from the bark *Austria*, wrecked here in 1887. Her anchor is the most noticeable remnant, but some pieces of hull, a bollard, and some chain also remain. She was a

Useful Addresses on the Olympic Peninsula

- Olympic Peninsula Travel Association
  c/o Washington State Ferries
  Seattle Ferry Terminal, Pier 52
  Seattle, WA 98104
- Olympic National Park
  600 East Park Ave.
  Port Angeles, WA 98362
- Olympic National Forest
  Federal Building
  Olympia, WA 98501

Chambers of Commerce

- P.O. Box 229, Bremerton, WA 98310
- P.O. Box 300, Forks, WA 98331
- Grays Harbor, P.O. Box 450, Aberdeen, WA 98520
- Gig Harbor/Peninsula, P.O. Box 1245, Gig Harbor, WA 98335
- P.O. Box 3206, Lacey, WA 98503
- P.O. Box 382, Ocean Shores, WA 98569
- Olympia-Lacey-Tumwater, P.O. Box 7249, Olympia, WA 98501
- Olympic North Beach, P.O. Box 562, Copalis Beach, WA 98535
- 1217 E. First, Port Angeles, WA 98362
- 2437 Sims Way, Port Townsend, WA 98368
- P.O. Box 1063, Poulsbo, WA 98370
- Sequim-Dungeness, P.O. Box 907, Sequim, WA 98382
- P.O. Box 666, Shelton, WA 98584

seaworthy vessel, 18 years old, 1,300 tons, and in able hands when a gale blew her ashore.

Sand Point is at the end of the trail that wends southwest from the Lake Ozette road.

This trail is usually the first leg for hikers making the 9-mile Ozette–Sand Point–Cape Alava triangle. Heading south from Sand Point turns the venture into a stouter hike. Though no walk for a novice, it is not hazardous to go all the way to Rialto Beach, at the mouth of the Quillayute River some 16 miles south.

The dedicated beach hiker will find the shore memorable for scenery, tidepools, and the guaranteed exertion of scrambling up and over one or more of the narrow headlands along the shore. A lucky traveler may spot a wild animal scouting the water's edge for food.

The hike is punctuated by memorials to three shipwrecks. The first of these, the Norwegian Memorial, is roughly west of the southern tip of Lake Ozette, about 8 miles south of Sand Point. (The easy way to reach the monument is by a boat taxi from the resort to the south end of the lake, where a 2-mile trail drops to the shore in exactly the right place.) The memorial marks the common grave of 18 men who perished in the wreck of the three-masted bark *Prince Arthur*, which mistook a cabin's light for that of Tatoosh Island and turned onto the rocks one January night in 1903.

The Chilean Memorial is 5 miles south of the Norwegian, just around the tip of Cape Johnson, and 3 miles north of Rialto Beach. It does double duty. The schooner *W.J. Pirrie* ran aground in November 1920, with 20 of 22 aboard drowning. Another Chilean vessel, the bark *Lenore*, grounded with lives lost 37 years earlier.

Rialto Beach and La Push. A paved road turns west from U.S. 101 about a mile north of the town of Forks and pursues a scenic way to the sea. Six miles inland the road divides. The north branch goes through Mora campground to Rialto Beach on the north side of the Quillayute River; the south branch goes to the resort town of La Push.

Rialto Beach is the center of national park activity in this part of the coastal strip. A good-size picnic ground is at the backshore. A particularly good smelt run takes place on the broad, sandy beach, which is also the roadhead for hikes north.

The National Park Service campground, Mora, has 91 sites well inland in sheltering woods. Motels flank the campground.

The temperate jungle

Rain forests are common in the tropics, but only the Olympics have created a large one in a cool climate.

La Push is a commercial and sport salmon harbor in the Quillayute (or Quileute) Indian Reservation. A low-key resort, it offers fine beaches.

The Indian residents of the town have retained their traditional skill with the dugout canoe. They paddle nimbly through seas that give veteran coast guardsmen the shudders. However, visitors are not required to use canoes; they go out in larger rental craft or aboard charter boats.

La Push also has fine beaches and is one endpoint of a superior 16-mile hike along the coast south. First Beach, adjoining the south jetty of the river in town, has a parking lot behind a tremendous tangle of driftwood. The south end is marked by a small, easily accessible sea cave.

Second Beach can be reached along the shore at low tide but is handier by way of a trail that joins the road into town. A tall offshore rock (known regionally as a "sea stack") close inshore and rugged Teawhit Head to the south make this beach one of the most scenic in the region.

Tidepools along Teawhit are rich with sea life.

Third Beach is accessible only by a 1-mile trail from La Push Road. (Teawhit Head cannot be rounded or climbed from Second Beach.) From a point near the south end of this secluded beach begins the difficult trail to Oil City, 15 miles south. Hikers must climb over several lofty headlands, slither along on seaweed-slicked boulders.

The south end of the beach trail is at Oil City— a name on a map, no more. U.S. 101 is 12 gravel-road miles inland.

On this beach hike and the more northerly one between Rialto and Ozette, hikers must carry maps and tide tables, go around heads only at low tides, and go over them on marked trails when tides are high or rising. Wise hikers check in at a ranger station before departing on either hike.

Kalaloch and Ruby Beach. This short stretch of shore is the northernmost at which a road parallels the shore. Kalaloch offers a sandy beach, a roomy lodge, and a 195-site campground right at the shore. Seven numbered beaches flank it—the first two to the south, the others to the north. Ruby Beach is just north of Beach Seven. All within 6 miles, these beaches offer a gentle yet fairly complete introduction to wilderness beaches. Kalaloch itself has some razor clams; Beach Two has fine driftwood; Beach Four has smelt.

U.S. 101 stays just far enough inland to be out of sight and out of mind. Hikes from highwayside parking lots to shore run half a mile or less. Once on one beach, a wanderer can walk easily to the next. Surf fishing is productive at all beaches.

Rain Forests

On the inland side of U.S. 101 the world is almost as wet as on the beach side. In the deep river valleys—the Quinault, Queets, and Hoh—local rain is supplemented by water coming down from the high peaks. As the valleys flatten, the water slows enough to create true climax rain forests—places so dense with vegetation that only a few trails can be kept open. Sitka spruce and Douglas fir grow to 275 feet, with 8-foot trunk diameters; mosses and ferns dominate a diverse forest understory.

Roads poke into all three of the river valleys.

Lake Quinault and the river above it are the most developed areas, under a cooperative administration of the national park, the Olympic National Forest, and the Quinault Indian Reservation.

The National Park Service administers the north shore, including a ranger station, a small visitor center, and the 31-site July Creek campground (for tents only). On the south side, the Forest Service has two campgrounds—Willaby (7 tent, 12 R.V. sites) and Falls Creek (21 tent, 5 R.V. sites)—a ranger station, and a rain forest interpretive display. Willaby and Falls Creek have beaches and boat launching ramps. Concessionaire campgrounds and lodges ring the lake; Quinault Lodge on the south side is the oldest and most famous. Amanda Park, in the Quinault Reservation at the west end of the lake, offers stores, gas stations, and other commercial services. The Quinaults control all use of the lake itself.

The two roads leading from U.S. 101 along the north and south shores of the lake continue through the rain forest well into the high country. A crossroad ties the two together near their eastern ends. The northern road ends at North Fork Campground (10 tent sites); the southern one goes to Graves Creek Campground (45 sites, open to trailers). These are departure points for top-of-the-world hikes across the Olympics. A National Park Service ranger is stationed at each campground.

The Queets River rain forest, a few miles north, is much less heavily used. An unpaved stub road ambles along the river, ending at the 95-site Queets Campground of the national park. It, too, is a departure point for high-country hikes.

The Hoh River rain forest is the northernmost geographically but falls in between the other two in terms of development. At the high end of a road on the north side of the river, the national park's 95-site Hoh Campground leads to high-country trails. The year-round visitor center has a museum and naturalist program. Outside the park boundary, commercial campgrounds dot the road. Other campgrounds are on the river's south bank and along U.S. 101 near the river.

River-runners familiar with other Western waterways will find rafting through a rain forest a much different experience. Icy and milky with glacial silt, the Queets River flows full between banks overhung by outstretched limbs of big-leaf maples and black cottonwood, their branches dangling with moss.

Bogachiel State Park, with 119 acres and about 40 campsites, is a useful base point for exploring the Bogachiel River valley, a few miles north of the Hoh. This valley is transitional—lusher than a typical Pacific Northwest forest but less overgrown than the climax rain forests to the south. The river can produce fine catches, particularly of sea-run cutthroat in autumn. Along its bank, relatively open, easy-going hiking trails penetrate high toward its headwaters within the national park.

The state park is just off U.S. 101, 6 miles south of the town of Forks. The principal trails run eastward from there, or from a stub road leading east from U.S. 101.

Though the Bogachiel has a special reputation for cutthroat trout, these coast-side rivers are legendary among winter steelheaders. At that season fishermen can not only harvest fish but also enjoy the rain forests when the lack of deciduous leaf makes them somewhat more open. Big wild animals come down to winter in the lowlands, and chances of seeing them are good.

Tame Beaches

For years the citizens of Grays Harbor had the sandy, razor clam-rich beaches north of the bay pretty much to themselves. In mobile modern times, however, visitors have outnumbered locals 100 to 1 when a favorable tide has brought 30,000 clammers running.

Although the harvest of clams varies from season to season, all these visitors have given rise to a substantial resort development north along the shore up to the Quinault Indian Reservation boundary.

Ocean Shores, on the north spit of Grays Harbor, is the largest of the resort communities. Up the coast, Ocean City, Copalis, Moclips, and Pacific Beach are older and quieter.

To such natural attractions as razor clamming, surf fishing, and beachcombing, the resorts have added offshore salmon fishing, golf, art galleries, and even an occasional splash of night life.

The beach proper is one long park, but except for Ocean City State Park and state-operated beach accesses in each town, the backshore is privately owned.

An amble-gaited stub road, State 109, branches west from U.S. 101 at Hoquiam to serve the region.

Ocean Shores started out in the 1960s. It has hundreds of rentable rooms (many on the beach), several restaurants, and a golf course. As elsewhere in the state, motor vehicles are allowed on the beach. Rented mopeds and pickup trucks zoom by beach strollers; the oncoming traffic is stopped only by soft sand. Carcasses of Plymouths as well as whales are to be discovered on this sandy strand.

The municipally owned golf course (18 holes; 6,021 yards; par 71) is flat and not heavily treed, but water makes it tougher than it looks.

A small fleet of charter boats is available for fishermen at the marina; a stable rents horses for beach rides; clammers can easily rent gear for digging.

Oyehut is a quieter, smaller extension of Ocean Shores, adjoining it on the north.

Ocean City State Park is on the local road that leads from State 109 into Ocean Shores; the park entrance is only a few hundred feet from the highway. The 140-acre park spreads out across low, rolling dunes. Most of its campsites (over 100, with about 30 hookups) are sheltered in scrub trees well back from the shore. A road goes west to the beach. This beach access is supplemented by several public access spots in Ocean Shores, and others at Oyehut and the town of Ocean City.

Ocean City, straddling the highway to the north, is primarily a sequence of vacation homes.

Copalis Beach, next in line to the north, is the oldest and best known of the resort towns in the north beaches. It has a mixture of motels and beach cottage resorts, restaurants, and private trailer-camper parks. Griffiths-Priday State Park offers picnic sites, trails, and a covered area. The region is great for beach combing.

Pacific Beach and Moclips. Pacific Beach, another 8 miles up the road, is more dramatically set than its neighbors to the south. Rocks begin to compete successfully with sand at this point. The town tucks under the lee of a bluff at the back of a deep cove. The south end of its beach is pinched off at a forested headland. Around the corner to the north, a long, narrow ribbon of dark, fine sand stretches as far as Moclips on the southern boundary of the Quinault Indian Reservation.

At Pacific Beach a concessionaire operates a campground at state park standards, in cooperation with the State Parks Department. The 9-acre site has over 100 campsites and 20 hookups. Pacific Beach and Moclips have several motels and resorts right on the beach. This is a razor clammer's beach in season and a drift hunter's beach all year, especially in winter.

A gravel road heading northeast from Moclips connects State 109 with U.S. 101.

Closing the Loop

Most treks across the base of the Olympic Peninsula go quickly. U.S. 12/State 8 encourages speedy travel with four-lane road all the way.

Between Grays Harbor and Olympia, the southern edge of the Olympic Mountains offers the remotest, yet gentlest, side of the range. For those with some time, Olympia, at the foot of Puget Sound, has much to recommend it.

Between Grays Harbor and Olympia

Along the way between the side-by-side towns of Aberdeen and Hoquiam on Grays Harbor and Olympia at the foot of Puget Sound, several pleasant parks invite casual visits, and some fairly remote mountainous country beckons people who like to get away from it all.

Aberdeen and Hoquiam. A strategic location, plus a sizable collection of motels, has made these twin towns on Grays Harbor a popular overnight stop for visitors to the Olympic Peninsula. Two mansions in Hoquiam have been restored. The Polson Museum, on U.S. 101 where it enters town, is filled with artifacts and pictures. Hoquiam's "Castle," up the hill on Chenault Street, has been furnished to re-create its original elegance.

Lake Wynoochee is for those with a strong desire to fish or get away from it all. The Corps of

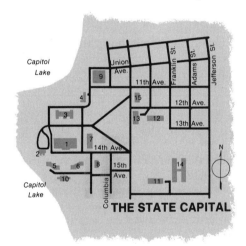

THE STATE CAPITAL

1 Legislative Building
2 Governor's Mansion
3 Temple of Justice
4 Greenhouse
5 Public Health Building
6 Public Lands Building
7 Insurance Building
8 Institutions Building
9 General Administration
10 State Library
11 Employment Security
12 Highways-Licenses
13 Archives and Records
14 Highway Building
15 Thurston County Courthouse

Engineers Visitor Center near Wynoochee Dam, well inside the Olympic National Forest, is 30 winding miles from Montesano. A 9-site campground is even higher up, at Wynoochee Falls.

Schafer State Park. Schafer hides away in foothills north of Satsop, on the Satsop River. The 119-acre park has 53 campsites (6 hookups), fishing, and swimming. Facilities also include sheltered kitchens and picnic tables.

Lake Sylvia State Park, 234 acres with about 40 campsites, attracts fishermen from afar, swimmers from nearby. Somewhat less remote than Schafer, it is just a mile north of Montesano.

Olympia, State Capital

Olympia attracts a great deal of attention from geography students and political figures as Washington's capital city. It attracts as much or more attention from gastronomes as home to incomparable oysters in bays north and south of town.

Accommodations. A brisk convention trade and political visitors have caused several large motels to be built in Olympia. The greatest cluster is along Capitol Way, off I-5 via Exit 105. The largest is right next to Exit 102.

Attractions in town. The great dome of the state legislature's Roman-Doric building dominates the city skyline. Inside the dome, a massive brass Tiffany chandelier hangs 185 feet above marble floors. During the legislative sessions, a myriad of activities fills the building. A narrated tour is available daily except holidays.

You can also tour the Governor's Mansion, next to the legislative building, but make arrangements with the tour office ahead of time—call (206) 586-TOUR.

Just south of the legislative building, the State Library houses sculpture, mosaics, and paintings by outstanding Northwest artists in addition to its large book collection.

The buildings that make up the "Capitol campus" are set in 55 lavishly landscaped acres. Great banks of rhododendrons blossom on the heels of flowering cherries in spring, the showiest season. A replica of Denmark's Tivoli Fountain provides a dramatic display of changing colors throughout the year. The five greenhouses that produce the plants are open to visitors; they're across from the sunken garden.

Capitol Way, the city's main street, runs along the east side of the grounds.

A block off Capitol Way at 211 West 21st Street, the State Capitol Museum, open weekdays, has a permanent collection of Northwest art as well as rotating exhibits. The handsome old mansion also houses a geologic survey of the state and oddments of pioneer history.

Parks and recreation. Olympia supports a sizable park system and offers excellent golf and tennis facilities.

Large parts of the city's waterfront and downtown have been renovated. Percival Landing Park added about 8 blocks of boardwalk (6 more to come) along the shore of the Sound. The park also brought sculpture, a 100-foot viewing tower, and a busy public moorage.

Capitol Lake Park, just below the capitol grounds, is a saltwater swimming stadium all summer long and a spawning route for salmon in mid-August. On shore, picnic grounds and a playground make the park a pleasant stopping point.

Priest Point Park, on Budd Inlet, is the city's largest picnic and recreation park. Reached on Easy Bay Drive, it has saltwater swimming beaches and nature trails as well as picnic areas.

Near Olympia. The Olympia Brewing Company in the neighboring town of Tumwater has a large plant next to I-5. Visitors are welcome to tour the spotless brewery and taste its end product. Tours run daily during normal business hours; Exit 103 gives direct access. Tumwater Falls Park, next to the brewery, is a handy picnic spot.

Oyster beds abound in Mud, Oyster, and Big and Little Skookum bays. The producers in the area will often give visitors a firsthand look at processing of the several kinds of oysters farmed there. The Olympia Oyster Company, the largest producer of the tiny, richly flavored native Olympia oyster, is open to visitors between 10 A.M. and 2 P.M. weekdays. To reach it, turn north off U.S. 101 onto the old Shelton Highway just north of Kennedy Creek Bridge. The Ellison Oyster Company gives tours by appointment; call (206) 866-7551.

The Mima Mounds Natural Area Preserve encloses 445 acres of regularly spaced hills approximately 7 feet high. The origin of the mounds is unknown, but an interpretive center describes the natural history of the area. Wildflowers can be viewed along self-guiding trails. The preserve is 13 miles south of Olympia via I-5. From Exit 95, it is 4½ miles further on State 121.

The Nisqually National Wildlife Refuge combines salt and freshwater marshes, tidal flats, forest, grasslands, swamps, and streams. It offers short trails, a boat launch, and a bird-watching platform. To reach the refuge, travel 10 miles east of Olympia on I-5 to Exit 114, then 1/2 mile north on Brown Farm Road.

A shoreline for hikers

The roadless Olympic National Park shore—more than 30 miles of it—offers visitors afternoon strolls or rugged 3-day hikes.

Mighty salmon, fast-digging
clams attract vacationers
to a gentle coastline

Southwest

Southwest Washington is two places—or, if not that, then two states of mind.

The coast from Grays Harbor south to the Columbia River mouth is a fine spot for deep-sea fishermen, razor clammers, drift hunters, winter wave watchers, and anybody else with a taste for salt water. Westport and the Long Beach Peninsula ask for—and get—crowds of visitors.

The inland valleys do no such thing; their excellent rivers and lakes are underpublicized and not at all crowded by fishermen, boaters, or campers. True, it takes a great deal of rain to keep all that greenery growing and all those rivers full. True, the woods are full of loggers and the fields of dairy and other farmers who do not favor frivolity. For both reasons, the region has considerable appeal for anyone seeking a day or two of calm outdoor relaxation.

Along Interstate 5, several tidy, attractive commercial centers offer civilized respite to the road-weary, along with some agreeably lively history.

Weather. The profile here follows that in the rest of western Washington, with not quite so many local quirks as areas farther north. The low hills of the coast ranges do not create dramatic rain forests or rain shadows as the Olympics do.

Average rainfall varies from 90 inches along the coast and the west-facing foothills down to 40 inches a year in the broad valleys. (Naselle, hard against the coast ranges on the Columbia River, is the regional champion with 114 inches.) Measurable precipitation comes on 160 to 180 days each year; about 50 days are cloudless. October through March is very gray and wet. July is the driest month—less than an inch of rain scattered over 5 days is typical.

Real heat is rare. In the warmest lowlands a typical year has only half a dozen days that reach the 90° range. Real cold is almost as rare. Some stations have never recorded a 0° reading, though inland frost comes 50 to 60 nights a year at lower elevations, more often at higher elevations.

Highways. The region has few major roads. The principal one is multilane Interstate Highway 5, relentlessly efficient carrier of north-south traffic.

Two-lane U.S. 101 also runs north-south, but closer to the coast than I-5. U.S. 12 arcs west from I-5 from a junction near Centralia to Aberdeen on Grays Harbor. Most major roads are wide and asphalt paved, with occasional uphill passing lanes. Expect to share any route other than I-5 with logging trucks.

As elsewhere in Washington, all federal and state highways carry green mile markers. On I-5 the numbers increase from south to north. The same is true of U.S. 101 from Megler to Aberdeen. On U.S. 12, mile 0 is at Aberdeen. On State Routes 4 and 6, however, numbers go up east to west.

The Southwest Coast

As the crow flies, Westport, at the mouth of Grays Harbor, is but 50 miles from Ilwaco, at the mouth of the Columbia River. However, the vast, oyster-laden shoals of Willapa Bay complicate matters.

Without the bay, the region would be a single long sandy beach with rolling, forested hills behind it. The bay gives variety to beaches and to the resort towns along them.

In practical terms, Westport and its environs put salmon first and razor clams second, while the Long Beach Peninsula reverses that order. Willapa Bay's contributions to the mix are oysters and sheltered water for small boats. Its nature makes the peninsula a perfect environment for cranberries and razor clams.

Westport

Until the late 1950s, Westport was a sleepy commercial fishing village just inside the south jetty of Grays Harbor. It had one pier with a packing shed, a Coast Guard Station, and a main street with two combination saloons and restaurants.

When offshore sport fishing for salmon boomed, Westport boomed with it. Now the boat basin houses a large collection of trim craft, and the waterfront street (formerly nonexistent) is a pro-

See additional map on page 65.

Corner

portionately long collection of charter offices, restaurants, and motels.

The atmosphere during the boom days was rough-hewn and hardy, even boisterous. This has changed in recent years. Many of the buildings on Westhaven, the waterfront street, have been renovated. The former Coast Guard station now houses both a maritime museum and the regional historical society. In a clear-walled display building are skeletons of a gray whale and other marine mammals. The two-story museum is open daily in summer, weekends in winter.

On a boat, the trip across the Grays Harbor bar can—and often does—make an average roller-coaster ride seem as stately as a boardwalk tour. The Columbia bar is more savage, but if the seas at Westport come in straighter, they do not come in much flatter. Hence the regulars here can eat a sandwich and drink coffee on a deck that changes planes by 45° every minute or two.

Downcoast at Grayland and beyond, razor clams are one attraction; cranberry bogs and the beautiful coastline contribute a sense of tranquility and peace.

Accommodations. The waterfront street in Westport has motels ranging from the very comfortable to dormitory-style accommodations. The interior of town holds several clusters of cottages. Grayland also has a number of beach cottage resorts. Overnight parks for campers are plentiful.

Attractions. Fishing charters are the main attraction. Salmon is king, and king salmon is the king of kings. For conservation reasons, the salmon season has been shortened, but the runs seem to be rebuilding. The charter fleet, forced to diversify, now offers excellent fishing for other species, including ling cod, rock cod, red snapper, halibut, and even shark. Whale watching and bird watching are also offered. A typical day trip on one of the 70-plus boats in the fleet costs slightly less than $45 without rental gear, slightly more with it. The Westport Charter Association, P.O. Box 654, Westport, WA 98595, provides a roster of members and other information on request.

Parks and recreation. Visitors have a choice of beach parks on this 12-mile stretch of coast.

Westhaven State Park runs from the jetty south to the old, deactivated Westport Light, where there is a second access road. This day-use area is a haunt for surf fishermen and drift hunters.

Twin Harbors State Park, 3 miles south of Westport on State 105, is the major camping park in the area. It has over 300 sites (about 50 hookups) tucked into a wooded area east of the highway. A picnic area, with kitchens and shelters, adjoins that and spills across to the beach side of the road.

Grayland State Park, another 3 miles south, is larger than Twin Harbors—401 acres compared to 172—but has only 60 hookup campsites to supplement its older neighbor to the north. The park has beach frontage backed by the camp and picnic areas in scrub growth along the backshore.

In addition to these, the state park system maintains two other beach accesses: one between Grayland and Twin Harbors parks, the other 3 miles south of Grayland on State 105.

Willapa Bay

Except for the sheltered side of the Long Beach Peninsula, Willapa Bay gets relatively little attention from visitors, and alas for those who miss a tranquil day in gentle beauty.

The less-settled parts of the bay's backshore offer visitors a chance to camp in handsome scenery and a good many chances to fish or picnic.

The lower bay. North of the Willapa National Wildlife Refuge headquarters, Highway 101's two county parks are augmented by several state-operated public fishing access sites. Neither park—Bush-Pacific (camping) or Bruceport (day use)—has suitable beaches for swimming or fishing, since the oyster beds are so near.

The town of Bay Center is an agreeable collection of piers and frame buildings surrounded by metal tubs, wire baskets, and other tools of the oystering trade.

The bountiful Pacific

Near the Columbia River's mouth (above), deep basalt sands hold rich crops of razor clams. Offshore (left) are salmon, schooling for their spawning runs. If the price for these prized catches of southwest Washington is hard work in tough conditions, reward to serious eaters is unbeatable.

South Bend. Oystering is the reason for South Bend, but there are other benefits to stopping in this little town besides fresh mollusks on the half-shell. A spruced-up downtown, an historical museum, and numerous benches welcome travelers in need of a rest. The town's premier architectural attraction is the Pacific County Courthouse, built in 1910 after a lively dispute over the site of the county seat. A small park with waterfall and duck pond is across the street from the courthouse—on Memorial Drive, two blocks up the hill from the bay.

The planted oyster beds in the bay are privately owned. (On public beds, visitors may take 18 oysters a day per person.)

Raymond, the next town along U.S. 101, tends to dairy farming, milling, and shipping. Attractions include a golf course and a handsome half-timbered library. North of Raymond one must go all the way to the bay mouth to find another access to shore, although State 105 from Raymond to Tokeland stays right with the unspoiled shoreline.

Tokeland itself is a small sport-fishing village. The place is so serene that the local bait shop rents crab rings so people can fish off the public dock if they are not of a mind to take a charter trip.

In addition to crabbing, Tokeland is a fine place for winter drift hunting. The road stops well short of the end of the spit, keeping all but the serious from collecting in the area. The rolling, forested hills across the bay provide a scenic backdrop.

Long Beach Peninsula

Except for Cape Disappointment and North Head, which loom up above the Columbia River mouth, the Long Beach Peninsula barely shows on topographic maps. It is 28 miles long, but few spots on the sandy spit reach 40 feet above sea level. The rich bounty from land and sea has been taken advantage of by some fine restaurants along the peninsula.

Accommodations. For a long time Long Beach and its peninsula neighbors stood as the kind of old-fashioned resort towns that made a body want to play the local nine-hole golf course in tweed knickers and cap. During the Gay 90s this was a favored retreat of Portlanders. A good many of the accommodations still are clusters of shingled beach cottages patterned on the venerable model. However, with the mid-1970s came several large new buildings.

Most of the new and many of the old resorts are in Long Beach and neighboring Seaview. Several miles north, the smaller towns of Klipsan and Ocean Park have their old-timey flavors intact.

Overnight camper parks thread throughout the area. In late autumn and winter, only a few resorts and camper parks stay open.

Attractions. The length of the peninsula, small towns alternate with long stretches of beach. At the base of State 103 is Ilwaco, pure fishing village—part commercial, part sport. In season, scores of salmon charters put out from its sheltered harbor to work the mouth of the Columbia River. This is a place for novices to leave the skippering to those who know the area. Though the Columbia bar has been tamed by dredges and jetties, it is still no place to get caught when the weather turns nasty. In the short history of navigation across the bar, more than 200 ships have been lost or damaged at a cost of more than 1,500 lives. The number of people lost in small boats runs a great deal higher. Ignorance of weather and wave conditions is doubtless the leading cause of tragedy.

Ilwaco also has a museum of frontier life, one block east of U.S. 101 on Lake Street.

Near Long Beach, Pioneer Road leads to two attractions: a large rhododendron nursery with gardens, and a university center for research on cranberry production. Free guided tours are available at the cranberry center; phone (206) 642-2031.

Toward the north end of the peninsula, two small oystering towns are worth a visit both by observers of rare industries and by photographers and water colorists who think highly of aging and picturesque architecture, both residential and marine. The towns, Nahcotta and Oysterville, can be reached from Ilwaco by Peninsula Road or from Long Beach via State 103 to Ocean Park, then east.

The canneries and smokehouses of Nahcotta welcome visitors in late fall and early winter, their active time. In summer there is very little oyster harvesting and therefore very little processing.

Just south of the oystermen's dock in Nahcotta, the Willapa Bay Shellfish Laboratory is open to visitors weekdays all year round. This is the place to learn about edible shellfish from the bay. Having learned, you can return to the dock to rent a skiff (power to be provided by the renter) and crab rings. Oysters are not for public picking, but they can be bought.

The town of Oysterville, which dates from 1854, is a national historic district.

Parks and recreation. After a fashion, the whole length of sandy beach from North Head to the tip of the spit is state park. At least it is all accessible through state-run access points—one at Seaview, one at Long Beach, one at Klipsan, three at Ocean Park, and one west of Oysterville.

This is the home of the razor clam in its season, as well as one of the richest beaches on the coast for winter combing in search of Japanese glass fishing floats.

Both may be found in or on 28 straight miles of basalt sand so fine that people can (and do) drive automobiles over it to get to the clam beds or the drift, or merely for the novelty. There is some excuse for cluttering up the beach with automobiles and crusting up the automobiles with salt: every time the jetties have been extended, the shore currents have retreated a corresponding distance, dumping their loads of sand that much sooner. Resorts that once were right next to the water (the hummocky ridge running all along the spit is the old backshore) now find themselves as much as half a mile away from it at high tide.

The technique for hunting razors is noted on page 20. Tough as that chore might be, serious beachcombing is tougher. Though the peninsula catches huge amounts of drift from the Japanese current in winter, most of it is snaffled off the beach by professionals before it comes to rest. The trick is to get up and follow the incoming highest high tide of the day, working along the edge of the surf.

Fort Canby State Park occupies a dip between Cape Disappointment inside the Columbia River mouth and North Head just outside.

The park has 250 campsites (60 hookups) tucked into a loosely set stand of birch just inside the main gate. Picnic sites for day users are up on North Head. To the east of the main gate is a boat launch.

Westward from the campsites, an asphalt road runs alongside the hulking stonework of the Columbia's north jetty. Toward the inner end of the jetty, a sandy beach encourages swimming in sun-warmed shoals, but the main event is another mile west. There a large parking lot gives access to a fishing platform on the jetty and to a beach good for both surf fishing and drift gathering. Veterans work the river side of the jetty for sea bass in winter and the ocean side for perch in summer. Surf fishermen work wave troughs north of the jetty for perch and other browsing species the year around.

This is also one of the fine vantage points in all the world for winter storm watching. On a blustery day, the Columbia bar is a seething mass of waves, the jetty a constant lash of spray.

Up on Cape Disappointment, fans of Lewis and Clark can spend hours in a fine interpretive center contemplating the epic journey of the great explorers. Rising up from some old gun emplacements, the center offers a solid retreat from heavy weather.

The expedition of 1805 had no such comfort when it arrived in the dead of winter to be greeted by a typical day: ". . . at two o'clock," reads the journal, "the flood tide set in, accompanied by a high wind from the south, which, about four o'clock, shifted to the southwest, and blew almost a gale directly from the sea. The immense waves now broke over the place where we were encamped, and the large trees, some of them 5 or 6 feet thick, which had lodged at the point, were drifted over our camp. We remained in the water and drenched with rain during the rest of the day."

The Cape Disappointment Coast Guard Station and Lighthouse, about 4 miles southeast of Ilwaco, is open to visitors on weekday afternoons and all day Saturday and Sunday. On a nearby promontory stands North Head Lighthouse.

Leadbetter Point State Park, clear at the other end of the peninsula from Fort Canby–Ilwaco, has a different appeal. The park starts out as sparse woods and slowly becomes open sand dunes. This is the place for long walks on unspoiled ocean or bay beaches, and maybe for a bit of dune sliding.

Peninsula Road (parallel to the more westerly State 103) runs north from Nahcotta to Oysterville, then turns west. From this leg, a bumpy dirt track leads north into Leadbetter Park.

Willapa National Wildlife Refuge adjoins Leadbetter Point State Park, occupying the tip of the peninsula. The refuge covers four other areas around Willapa Bay: two at the southern edge of the bay, one on the eastern shore, and the last on Long Island. This island, 6 miles long and only 400 yards off the shore of Willapa Bay at its southern tip, can be reached only by private boat. On the island are seven marine campsites with picnic tables, 20 miles of woodsy trails, an old-growth cedar grove, and—for company—otters, raccoons, and some 200 species of waterfowl and shore birds. (March is the peak month for bird-watching.) Before going to the island, check in at the refuge headquarters on U.S. 101, 12 miles northeast of Ilwaco. The headquarters itself is worth a visit for its display ponds of Canada geese and other birds.

The Columbia River Mouth

State 4 slips west from Longview toward the mouth of the Columbia, 75 miles distant. Except for a hilly stretch in the middle, State 4 and its branch, State 401, hug the bank of this busiest stretch of river.

Cathlamet, an early-day logging town, has arrived in the present with a distinct flavor, owing in one way to the complete absence of fast-food franchises and in another to the presence on Main

Street of an elegantly restored old hotel.

Within walking distance of downtown is a traditional Pacific Northwest town park, a woodsy place with a sheltered cookhouse, horseshoe pits, a ball field, and—a modern addition—two excellent lighted tennis courts.

Near town the nine-hole, 2,641-yard, par 35 Skyline Golf Course threads through tall conifers.

From Cathlamet, a bridge crosses to Puget Island; from the opposite side of the island, a small car ferry runs a quick course to Westport, Oregon.

A few miles east of Cathlamet, Countyline Park is the place for bank fishermen. In season its long sandy beach is stuck full of poles whose owners hope—with some reason—for salmon. (Sturgeon fanciers gather on a steeper shore a mile or so east, opposite large piers on an island.) The day-use park, administered jointly by Cowlitz and Wahkiakum counties, also has picnic tables.

Boaters can get onto the river from public launching ramps a mile east of Skamokawa and on Brooks Slough.

Skamokawa (locally pronounced Ska-*mock*-away), though not Venice, sits on a slough-crossed plain that makes getting around town in a boat as easy as using a car—or easier. Observers of marine architecture will find all sorts of quirky design.

Collectors of covered bridges can look up one of Washington's rare survivors at Grays River, on a local road just west of Skamokawa and just south of State 4.

Fort Columbia State Park, 2 miles west of the Astoria-Megler toll bridge, is now a serene picnic park and historic museum after a quiet career as a shore battery post protecting a river that was never invaded. The 592-acre park has virtually the only swimming beach on the Columbia below Vancouver, except for one right at the mouth.

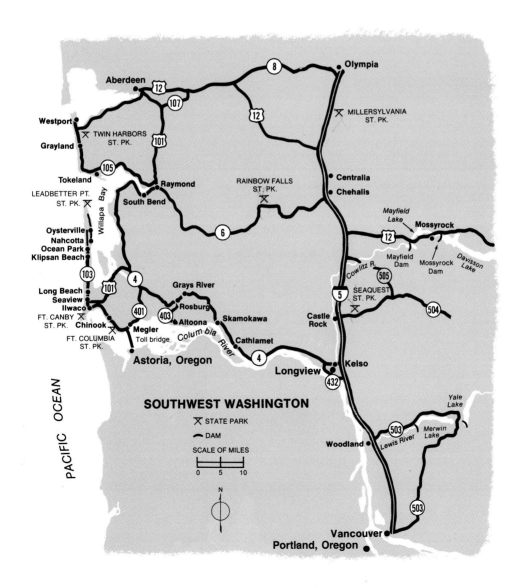

SOUTHWEST WASHINGTON

X STATE PARK

⌐ DAM

SCALE OF MILES

0   5   10

N

The nearby town of Chinook has a riverbank camping park used mostly by fishermen. An adjoining boat launch operated by the Port of Chinook charges a small fee. Several modest motels amplify the overnight possibilities.

Ilwaco, at the river mouth, already has been noted on page 63.

I-5: Twin Cities and Volcano Access

For whatever curious reason, cities along the major highway of southwest Washington tend to come in pairs: Portland-Vancouver (forgiving a state boundary), Longview-Kelso, and Centralia-Chehalis.

Some smaller single municipalities are interspersed along I-5, but the paired towns generally offer the widest range of accommodations and diversions for anyone so wearied by the relentlessness of freeway driving that an hour's stop is the minimum.

This southern stretch of I-5 also gives access to Mount St. Helens via roads following river courses up into the Cascade Mountains. The volcano is visible from several points; flights over the devastated areas are available.

Vancouver

Vancouver is Washington's oldest continuously settled city. Its present role is as an extension of the sprawling Portland metropolitan area, but lively legacies of Hudson's Bay Company traders and U.S. Grant's tour as a U.S. Army officer lead the way in making this town one of Washington's best for strolling with famous shades of the past.

Accommodations. Most of Vancouver's large, modern motels are in the downtown area west of I-5, from the riverfront north to 13th Street. Smaller clusters of motels are at NE 78th Street (Exit 4 from the freeway) and also along old U.S. 99 north of that road.

Attractions. In this historic Washington city, the major points of interest come from the past. A freewayside information center a few hundred feet north of the Interstate Bridge gives directions to the highlights, which form a tight circle near downtown on both sides of the freeway.

Fishing fleet at rest

Ilwaco, inside the Columbia River mouth, is—with Westport—a major harbor for charter boats.

Fort Vancouver was a Hudson's Bay Company trading post founded in 1825. It peaked in the 1840s on the site where its reconstruction now stands. Within that decade, the American colonials prevailed over English attempts along the Columbia River. A United States Army post came to occupy the same long, gentle slope leading down to the river.

The reconstructed trading post, an interpretive center explaining it, and the officers' row of the army post form the nucleus of Vancouver's early-day attractions. All may be reached from the Mill Plain Exit, 1C, from the freeway.

Officers' row, a fine demonstration of the fact that rank does have its privileges, sits highest on the slope. The oldest of its houses, dating to 1849, is a museum dedicated to Ulysses S. Grant, who kept office hours there as a rising young brevet major. The museum, containing Grant memorabilia, is open daily.

Not far downslope, a National Park Service interpretive center explains much about fur trading and other aspects of daily life in the Hudson's Bay Company stockade. The center is open daily. A children's playground and some picnic tables adjoin, all with an overview of the fort.

The fort proper is a painstaking restoration of the log stockade, corner blockhouse, and some of the interior buildings. Fans of western movies will recognize the architecture instantly, though serious fantasizing about 1846 comes hard because a busy airport is right next door.

On the other side of the freeway, in the present downtown, is the Clark County Historical Museum at 16th and Main. It has among its exhibits a re-creation of a pioneer doctor's office. The museum is open afternoons, Wednesday through Sunday.

Local pioneers of wealth are represented by the nearby Slocum House at Sixth and Esther. Now a theater, the magnificent building was originally a private residence. It points up the fact that a widow's walk could be as appropriate on the house of a Columbia River–based seafarer as on any New Englander's.

On a more modest scale, Covington House at 4201 Main was an early log-cabin schoolhouse. It is open Tuesday through Thursday in the summer.

Small specialty shops occupy the 1873 brick building that formerly housed the Providence Academy; it is at 400 East Evergreen.

Parks and recreation. Several major units of the municipal park system weave among the historic points of interest.

Esther Short Park, flanking Slocum House in the downtown, is a superior elaboration on the traditional plaza park. Mature trees shade most of its 5 acres of picnic tables and playground equipment. The park also has ample playfields.

On the other side of the freeway near the Mill Plain Boulevard exit—the same one that leads to Fort Vancouver—are two versatile parks, George C. Marshall (11 acres with an indoor swimming pool and picnic tables) and City College (with a lengthy fitness course).

Vancouver has several public golf courses. Vancouver Lake is a favorite spot for biking, boating, swimming, and picnicking.

Woodland and the Lewis River

The little town of Woodland is the center of a farming, dairying, and poultry-raising area. Near it is the Lewis River's placid junction with the Columbia—only 60 miles from the river's tumbling headwaters on Mt. Adams. Within that short span are white water for kayaking, three big pools behind as many dams, and finally, a slow floater's paradise. A steelheaders' river where it races, the Lewis is voluminous enough for sailboaters where it has been stilled.

The Lewis runs close along one flank of Mount St. Helens; State 503 leads to the Yale information Station at the southwest corner of the volcanic monument.

Klager Lilac Gardens, the former estate of Hulda Klager, is 1½ miles west of I-5 at the Woodland exit, 21. The 4½ acres display a variety of perennials and other plants. The many kinds of lilac, some of them hybridized by Hulda, bloom around the first two weeks of May. The gardens are open daily, and house tours are available by appointment; call (206) 225-8996.

Indian History in Washington

The same variable climate that makes contemporary Washington such a diverse economic and recreational region also made it home to a richly varied range of Indian societies.

The coastal Indians lived very much with saltwater. Their primary transportation was by boat. Their principal foods were salmon and other fish and shellfish. Through the bleak, wet winters, they lived in immense, permanent longhouses constructed of wood.

In the interior were tribes that lived much more in the fashion of the plains Indians. They were skilled horsemen and hunters of mammals. The tepee was a common shelter.

People with an interest in history extending back beyond European colonizers can find rich resources in Washington. Besides the large collections, each of the historical museums found in many of the towns throughout the state has its own trove of Indian artifacts.

In Seattle, the Daybreak Star Arts and Cultural Center in Discovery Park displays a fine art collection in a building with a dramatic, timbered interior. The landscape outside the building includes the Great Circle, Lance and Shield Plaza, Reflecting Ponds, and Serpent Mound. The center is open daily; call (206) 285-4425 for information.

Also in Seattle, the Burke Museum at the 45th Street entrance to the University of Washington houses a dramatic collection of totem poles and other Indian pieces. Masks and other artifacts are part of the Seattle Art Museum's permanent collection; the Pacific Science Center has a reconstructed longhouse.

Trips to Tillicum Village on Blake Island depart from Seattle's Pier 56. At the island are Indian-style baked salmon, costumed dance performances, and craftwork. Call (206) 329-5700.

Further west, two museums on reservation lands are worth visiting. The Suquamish Museum, overlooking Agate Passage between Bainbridge Island and Poulsbo, has photographs, artifacts, and recorded interviews. It is open daily in summer; call (206) 598-3311.

At the very northwestern tip of the Olympic Peninsula, the Makah Cultural and Research Center displays artifacts—some of them 2,000 years old—from a coastal archaeological site. These Indians hunted whales with their ocean-going dugout canoes; a canoe replica, as well as a 60-foot cedar longhouse, can be seen here. Call (206) 645-2711.

In the central part of the state, the Yakima Indian Nation Cultural Center is just off U.S. 97 near Toppenish. Shaped like a stylized winter lodge, the dramatic building is visible from a distance. Inside are a restaurant, museum, library, movie theater, and gift shop. The Yakima Indians produce beadwork that is sold here along with jewelry made from Ellensburg blue, a semiprecious stone. Contact the center at (509) 865-2800 for information.

In Spokane, MONAC (Museum of Native American Cultures) is entirely devoted to Indians of the Americas; call (509) 326-4550. Also in Spokane, Cheney Cowles Memorial Museum presents a well-curated Indian collection.

Cedar Creek grist mill, a classic example of a pioneer mill, provides a change of pace. The crude structure, dating from 1876, is 9 miles east of Woodland via County Road 16, then left another mile along Grist Mill Road.

Merwin Lake is a reservoir just 10 miles off I-5; from Exit 21, State 503 leads straight to it. In the lowlands, Merwin Park is a picnic and swimming park with room for 2,000 people. Close to Merwin Dam, it has sheltered picnic stoves. Speelyai Bay Park, 11 miles uplake, also has picnic sites and swimming; a boat ramp and service area have made it a favorite of power boaters.

On Yale Lake, along Lewis River Road, Yale and Cougar parks provide picnicking and swimming. Yale also has a boat launch. At the upper end of the lake are Cougar Camp and Beaver Bay parks.

A number of the park and recreation developments along the Lewis are operated by Pacific Power. For current information on beaches and picnic parks, write: Pacific Power Recreation Department, Public Service Building, Portland, OR 97204.

Along the east fork of the Lewis River are three more parks.

Lewisville County Park is 3 miles north of the town of Battle Ground, just east of State 503. A 640-acre woodland, it has space for picnickers and offers swimming beaches, playgrounds, and walking trails.

Battle Ground Lake State Park, cupped in the crater of a long-extinct volcano, has 50 campsites and several concessionaires, including boat rentals. The park's attractions are fishing and hiking. It is northeast of Battle Ground on a local road. In the town of Battle Ground, 2½-hour scenic train rides are available; call (206) 687-7428.

Close to where the Lewis River crosses I-5, 18 miles north of Vancouver at Exit 16, Paradise Point State Park offers campers 70 campsites plus a few primitive and walk-in tent sites. The park is the termination point for float trips.

Longview-Kelso

Longview and Kelso occupy the point where Interstate 5 and the Columbia River part company, the freeway continuing north while the river bends west to meet the Pacific Ocean.

Longview sprang into existence all of a piece in 1923 as one of the West's earliest planned cities. The founders of this logging and milling town chose a riverbank site that could—and does—provide a major deep-water port, and they took pains to design handsome residential neighborhoods well away from the mills.

Neighboring Kelso, older but smaller, serves as the Cowlitz County seat and as a retail center.

Abundant smelt, steelhead, and sturgeon make it a fishing and canning center.

Accommodations. Kelso, split by Interstate 5, has several major motels clustered near Exit 39. Most of Longview's motels are near the hub formed by 15th and Washington, the west edge of the main business district. The area is accessible from I-5 exits 36 and 39.

Attractions. Visible from Interstate-5 before you reach the towns, Trojan Nuclear Power Plant has a visitor center that is open Wednesday through Sunday. Call (503) 556-3751 for directions.

The Reynolds Metals Company offers tours of its aluminum reduction plant Thursdays at 1 P.M. Tollycraft, the boat builder, gives tours of its Kelso plant by appointment.

The Cowlitz County Museum, near the county courthouse in Kelso, includes a reconstructed log cabin among its souvenirs of local pioneers and Indians. The building is just off State 4 in the middle of town. Exit 39 leads past it from I-5. A tourist information stop is at Exit 39.

Parks and recreation. Kelso has several parks within easy access of the freeway.

In Longview, Lake Sacajawea Park's tree-shaded rolling lawns stretch more than a mile, flanking a narrow ribbon of water. The lawns in turn are flanked by private gardens lush with rhododendrons. Their bloom time, May, is dazzling.

Picnic tables dot the lawns and some lakeside terraces. Bicycle/jogging trails wind all through the park. There is no swimming, but the water is perfect for lazy summer rowing in small rental boats.

Just to the north, John Null Park has lighted tennis courts, a playground, and picnic tables. It is just off Ocean Beach Highway (State 4) via Pacific Street.

Mint Valley Municipal Golf Course (18 holes; 6,017 yards; par 71) is fairly level but has lots of sand and water. It is north of State 4 via 38th Street, well west of downtown Longview.

Access to Mount St. Helens

The best starting point for a trip to the national volcanic monument is the visitor center on State 504, just east of I-5 and Castle Rock. To reach it, take Exit 49 from I-5. (For more information, see page 81.)

The Volcanic Monument Visitor Center is next to Silver Lake at Seaquest State Park (54 tent sites and six hookups). Inside it you can view, among other attractions, a film of the May 1980 explosion. Maps, brochures, and other information are available here. Trails and road tours give visitors a close-up view of the grumbly mountain.

The **Toutle River,** which parallels State 504 as it heads toward the volcano, has quite a deposit of volcanic ash along its banks. It was once a premier steelhead and salmon stream, and the fish are returning to its silt-laden waters.

Cowlitz River

Like the Lewis, the Cowlitz River in its free-running days was turbulent in the upper reaches, placid in the lower ones. With the coming of Mayfield and Mossyrock dams, it too has begun to be developed in its ballooned middle as a recreational resource.

U.S. 12 branches east from I-5 at Exit 68, 9 miles south of Chehalis. It provides ready access to Lake Mayfield and its neighbor, Davisson Lake.

With 454 acres, Kinswa State Park on Mayfield Lake has about 100 campsites and 40 hookups tucked into fir forest. A boat-launching ramp accompanies them. The picnic grounds and a lawn-backed swimming beach are a separate unit some hundreds of yards west. The swimming beach is in a shallow lagoon fenced off from the main lake. Walking trails ramble all through the park. The park is reached by a loop road north of U.S. 12.

Lower in the Cowlitz River Valley and well away from water, Lewis & Clark State Park is a 533-acre property devoted principally to picnickers, especially groups. It does have 25 campsites. It is on old U.S. Highway 99, the Jackson Highway, not far south of that road's junction with U.S. 12 and only 5 miles from I-5.

A mile nearer the freeway, also on the Jackson Highway, is Jackson Courthouse, a pioneer structure restored as a heritage site.

Centralia-Chehalis

The tidy, attractive town of Centralia is the major commercial center for timber and dairying communities in the broad, rolling Cowlitz Plain. Chehalis, two miles south, is both the Lewis County seat and a manufacturing town.

In addition to Centralia's being a useful stopover point on Interstate 5, the twin towns are close to the Cowlitz River, known for its smelt runs.

Accommodations. A major concentration of motels flanks I-5 at the north side of Centralia, Exit 82. A smaller number are at Exit 81, southwest of the main business district.

Attractions, parks, and recreation. The town of Chehalis houses the Lewis County Historical Museum, located in the old railway depot. In Chehalis (next to city hall) is a National Rose Test Garden. Also available for touring is the Centralia Steam-Electric Plant.

Fort Borst Historic Park adjoins the freeway on the west, two blocks from Exit 82. It has a fortlike log blockhouse reconstructed so long ago it looks like the original, an arboretum, a kids-only fishing lake, playground equipment, a steam locomotive, cooking shelters, and lots of picnic tables under tall conifers. Just west of the woodsy community kitchen lies a complex of sports fields.

Eighteen miles east of Chehalis along State 6, Rainbow Falls State Park has 50 campsites and a small stand of virgin cedar, fir, and hemlock.

North of the two towns, leave I-5 at Exit 88a (Tenino) to reach Wolf Haven, a sanctuary for more than 30 wolves. For a small fee, visitors can take an hour-long, guided walking tour. Call (206) 264-2775 for hours and directions.

Useful Addresses in Southwest Washington

- Fort Vancouver National Historic Site Vancouver, WA 98661
- Mount St. Helens National Volcanic Monument, Gifford Pinchot National Forest, 500 W. 12th St., Vancouver, WA 98660
- Tourist Information, P.O. Box 128, Longview, WA 98632

Chambers of Commerce

- P.O. Box 366, Battle Ground, WA 98604
- Cathlamet Commercial Club P.O. Box 52, Cathlamet, WA 98612
- Twin Cities, P.O. Box 666, Chehalis, WA 98532
- Columbia Pacific Visitor Bureau, P.O. Box 562, Long Beach, WA 98631
- P.O. Box 58, Kelso, WA 98626
- 1563 Olympia Way, Longview, WA 98632
- P.O. Box 726, Tenino, WA 98589
- 404 E. 15th St., Suite 4 Vancouver, WA 98660
- Westport-Twin Harbors, P.O. Box 306, Westport, WA 98595

Graveyard of the Pacific
North Head light looks into the Columbia River mouth, perilous for ships but pleasing to see.

In these mountains for
all seasons, Rainier is but
one peak among hundreds

The Cascade

The Cascades are mountains to behold in a dozen different lights.

Awesome products of volcanic fire and glacial ice, they come as towering single peaks and in steep-walled, glacier-scoured rows. The Cascades also come as soft, rolling foothills and huge alpine meadowlands.

It is a fair truth to say that eight seasons of weather sweep across the Cascades, so different are the climates on the east slopes from those on the west.

The uses of these singularly diverse mountains are almost without limit. Fishing can be a year-round occupation. Lowland hiking trails also stay open through the winter, although midsummer in the high country brings out hikers and campers in their greatest numbers. Summer is also the season for mountaineering on a remarkable variety of rock and ice—some of it among the most difficult technical terrain in North America, some within the reach of aging beginners. In winter, deep snows provide a base for downhill and cross-country skiers, and snowshoers.

Nearly all of the high Cascades country is federal parkland. So too is much of the foothill region. Mt. Rainier National Park is the star of the show, the most visible and most visited mountain park in the region. Mount St. Helens National Volcanic Monument is the newest major attraction. The rest of the roster includes North Cascades National Park, plentiful wilderness areas, and dozens of smaller recreational developments in the national forests that surround the formal parks.

A general progression from rounded contours and relatively low elevations in the south to fierce heights in the north marks the march of the Cascades through Washington. The great row of isolated volcanoes starts with Mt. Adams and the dramatically rekindled Mount St. Helens in the south, proceeding northward with Mt. Rainier (highest of them all at 14,410 feet), then Shuksan and Baker near the British Columbia border. Impressive as these giants are by themselves, they do not separate climate and economy into east

and west Washington. The great wall of the main range does that.

All this tends to make the Cascades sound remote to any but dedicated outdoorsmen. However, the reverse is true. Four major mountain highways allow close looks at striking scenery to the most sedentary of auto tourists. Well-maintained paved highways also reach well into the two national parks. Strung out along the pass roads are some of the state's most picturesque small towns.

Weather. This great, unbroken ridgepole of mountains sharply divides the climate of Washington state into the wet west and the dry east. The slopes themselves make up two more climate regions. In general effect, the west side exaggerates what goes on in the lowlands below, while the east slopes show a somewhat moderated form of the drier basin beyond.

Stampede Pass (just south of Snoqualmie Pass, a few miles off Interstate Highway 90), at a 4,000-foot elevation, gives a fair hint at westside weather. On the average, it is cloudy 241 days a year; precipitation falls on 206, with 85 of those days snowy. The annual total precipitation averages 92 inches a year, although the accumulated snow can reach a depth of 450 inches. Only 70 days are clear. On 190 nights a year the minimum temperature is 32°F. or less; on 94 days the maximum is freezing or below. The highest temperature on record is 90°F.

Ellensburg, a few miles east at 1,727 feet, has dramatically different weather: 156 cloudy days in a year, but 110 clear ones. The annual precipitation is 8.86 inches; snow depth runs to a total of 31 inches. On 21 summer days the temperature tops 90°F.; in winter, 155 overnight lows are at freezing or lower, while 27 daily highs fail to warm to 32°F.

A howling rainstorm can come along at any time, though July and August are more reliably fair than other months. The first lingering westside snows come at higher elevations in September, work down to 3,000 feet by the last of October, and reach the 1,500-foot mark by mid-

See additional maps on pages 76, 81, and 88.

Mountains

winter. Dates on the east slopes lag 2 weeks or so behind this schedule. Maximum accumulated depths are usually in March at the 3,000-foot level and up. In typical years, snow does not clear off elevations over 5,000 feet before mid-July.

Highways. Four Cascade pass highways make a rickety-looking ladder with I-5 and U.S. 97 as the north-south legs. Their characteristics are diverse indeed. From north to south the roads are:

• The North Cascades Highway, officially State 20, is the most spectacular. Opened in 1972, the often narrow two-lane road connects the northern Puget Sound basin with the Methow and Okanogan Valleys between early spring and late fall. Heavy snows close it for the winter. Slow, noncommercial, beautifully scenic, it can be combined with the Stevens Pass Highway to make a loop.

• The Stevens Pass Highway, U.S. 2, joins Everett on the west with Wenatchee on the east. Most of the road is two wide lanes, but near the summit several sections of divided four-lane highway ease traffic a good deal. Pleasure drivers share the road with a considerable volume of commercial traffic, especially logging trucks on the west side. The scenery is almost as spectacular as that on the North Cascades route.

• The Snoqualmie Pass Highway, Interstate 90, is the workhorse road. The route has four lanes all the way from Seattle to Chicago. Much of it is divided, but a few spots in the higher reaches are not. Traffic is frequently intense. This is the main route for truckers, but it remains fast. In winter it is quickest to be plowed free of snow.

• The White Pass Highway, U.S. 12, is the southernmost mountain pass route, connecting the southwest corner of the state with Yakima. Except for some spectacular views of Mt. Rainier and one brief but glorious gorge, the up-close scenery is appealing more than awesome. A two-laner, its pace is leisurely.

The softened outlines of the Cascades toward the southern margin of Washington allow for some branch routes off White Pass Highway. A northward jog along State 123 to U.S. 410—the Chinook Pass Highway—offers a steeper, more scenic alternate route into the Yakima Valley. This route closes with the winter snows.

Mt. Rainier

People who have seen all the big mountains do not become blasé about Mt. Rainier. Rising almost 2 miles above surrounding foothills, this all-by-itself mountain is a stunning sight. Rivers of ice pour from its dazzling summit. Wrinkled glaciers grind through immense amphitheaters. Waterfalls drop feathery plumes into shadowy canyons. Snowfields sweep down like great wings to a base more than 100 miles around.

In a region famous for snowy volcanoes, this colossus of fire and ice holds all the records: biggest single glacier and largest glacier system (almost 50 square miles) in the U.S. excluding Alaska, highest volcanic summit (14,410 feet) in the lower 48 states, greatest snowfall ever recorded anywhere in the world (93.5 feet at Paradise ranger station in 1972).

Rainier is so big it makes its own weather, is visible from almost every major Washington city, and, in a land rich with peaks, is known simply as The Mountain.

But statistics are a poor measure; this is a mountain to be seen and experienced first-hand. For any traveler who can get to the Puget Sound basin, there is no problem. Rainier's glaciers are the most accessible in the nation.

All of the soaring peak and much of the surrounding foothill country lie within well-developed Mt. Rainier National Park. Recreational developments in flanking sections of Snoqualmie and Gifford Pinchot national forests supplement the national park.

Mt. Rainier National Park

Mt. Rainier National Park offers itself equally to auto tourists, day hikers, back-country campers,

Mountain for all seasons

Mt. Rainier was not named to describe its weather. Still, on a scale of rainy, rainier, and rainiest, it approaches the high end even in midsummer. Veteran hikers know this and come prepared (left). However, July and August are months of frequent sunshine (above). Day hikers and campers flock to the national park's hundreds of miles of trails to revel in tonic air.

and ice climbers. Winter use is somewhat less intense, but the activities are attractive nonetheless.

The accessibility almost cannot be exaggerated. Fine roads nearly loop the park, but at the same time they are a reasonably direct alternate route to I-5. Seattle is but 70 miles away. The grand circle tour can be done from Seattle in 9 hours—a tour bus does it daily in summer.

Auto touring. U.S. 12—the White Pass Highway—cuts away from I-5 just south of Chehalis, at Exit 68. Its looping course almost touches the southeast corner of the park at its junction with State 123. State 123 works along the park's eastern boundary to a junction with State 410. The latter route continues northward beyond the park. Before U.S. 12 meets State 123, State Route 7 (then 706) branches away from it toward the southwest corner of the park. There, from the Nisqually entrance, national park roads loop east to a junction with State 123 near Ohanapecosh.

Along these roads are the park's major visitor centers, lodges, and campgrounds.

Longmire, in the southwest quarter, is park headquarters. At a 2,761-foot elevation, the area has a national park inn and a visitor center. It also is the head of a network of gentle hiking trails.

Paradise, 13 miles east and much higher at 5,400 feet, is the park's best-known visitor area and its only all-year attraction. It has wildflowers in abundance in July and August, a display of autumn color in September, and as much as 30 feet of accumulated snow in April. Several day hikes depart from the area around the old Paradise Inn (open through the first week in October), giving superior close-up views of Nisqually glacier as one reward. This is also the launch point for the climbs—to Camp Muir at 10,000 feet or to the summit.

In winter, Paradise is open weekends only as a day-use cross-country ski and snow-play area.

Two of the park's five campgrounds are on the road between the Nisqually entrance and Paradise. Sunshine Point (18 sites) is at the entrance. Cougar Rock (200 sites) is about halfway between Longmire and Paradise.

Ohanapecosh, at a 1,900-foot elevation on State 123, is in deep forest alongside the Ohanapecosh River. Its particular allure is a population of native trout in a stretch of water open only to fly fishermen. Also of interest is the nearby Grove of Patriarchs, a forest 1,000 years old. A handful of gentle trails and a host of steep ones begin here in the southeast corner of the park.

Except for a 205-site National Park Service campground, Ohanapecosh has no overnight accommodations. Just outside the park are several National Forest Service campgrounds, and a number of motels and private campgrounds are in the town of Packwood (see page 78).

Sunrise, at 6,400 feet, is the highest point on park roads. On a 17-mile spur road off State 410, the area has a visitor center with displays explaining the volcanic history of Mt. Rainier. Located at the tree line, it is surrounded by alpine meadows rich with wildflowers.

The visitor center gives close views of Emmons Glacier and the snowy crest of Rainier. It is also an excellent vantage for watching climbers on difficult technical terrain. A skein of easy walks takes visitors closer to the major views.

Sunrise has walk-in picnic sites, a ranger station, visitor center, and snack bar. A campground with 10 sites is a half-mile walk away. Not far as the crow flies, but several miles distant on a separate spur road, is the 117-site White River Campground. Both camping areas are open only during the summer.

Rainier for day hikers. To appreciate Rainier's endless variety fully is to do some walking . . . on a high ridge where the roar of ice tumbling down from a glacier into a canyon can well up in engulfing waves . . . in an alpine garden as breezes ripple a sea of wildflowers . . . beside a glacier-fed stream clear and cold in the shade of trees 300 feet tall.

This park has hardly a corner that cannot be reached in a day hike. Partly this is because of the network of good roads, but the relatively small size of the park—378 square miles—is the key.

Along with the limited size there is the gigantic factor of the great snowy cone in the middle, which leaves the encircling band of forest and meadow only 5 miles wide on the average.

Within that band are 305 miles of marked trail. Some of those miles remain buried under snow for years on end. Many more are clear for only a short season, leaving limited opportunities in spring and fall. However, the summer possibilities are extensive.

The following is a roster of relatively short, easy hikes in each quarter of the park.

Four are in the northeast quarter.

Crystal Lakes trail runs east from State 410. A 3-mile hike gaining 2,300 feet of elevation, it ranges through forests into alpine meadows. Two lakes are on the route; elk and goats may be also.

Of the dozens of trails to choose from in the Sunrise area, one goes up 2,500 feet in 3¼ miles from the Sunrise parking lot to 7,800-foot Burroughs Mountain and dreamlike views of Winthrop and Emmons glaciers.

The 3-mile Glacier Basin trail starts at White River Campground and leads up 1,400 feet to spectacular flower fields.

Summerland Trail starts from White River Road 3 miles back toward State 410 from the campground. It gains 1,500 feet over 4 miles en route to great views of Little Tahoma, an 11,700-foot side peak that was merely the main slope of a much

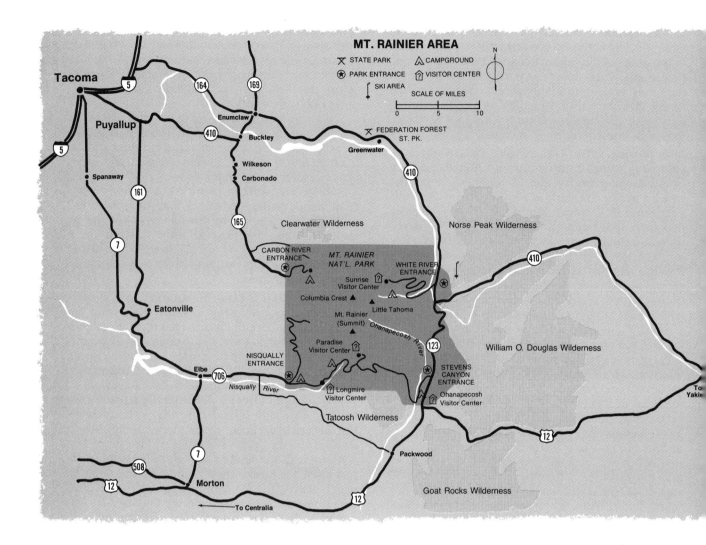

larger mountain until volcanic blasts blew the original lid off.

At Ohanapecosh in the southeast corner, the 3-mile Silver Falls Loop is a favorite hike, especially when storms sweep the exposed high country. The trail gains only 300 feet of elevation in its course through heavy forest. The trailhead is at the Ohanapecosh visitor center parking lot.

A few miles west via Stevens Canyon Road, Cowlitz Divide Trail climbs 2,000 feet in 3 miles. Most of the hike is on an open ridge much favored by elk. The trail starts at Box Canyon parking lot, 10 miles west of State 123.

Panorama Point is a 4½-mile loop trail from the parking lot at Paradise up through fine flower fields to some glorious views of glacier icefalls. The chances for solitude are much greater here than along the paved strollers' paths in the meadows surrounding Paradise.

Van Trump Park Trail climbs 1,900 feet in 2½ miles to Comet Falls, at 320 feet the highest waterfall in the park. Along the way are views of flow-

ers, falls, and often goats. The trail starts at Christine Falls parking lot, about midway up Paradise Road from the Nisqually entrance at the park's southwest corner.

Two hikes launch out from West Side Road, which branches off Paradise Road just inside the Nisqually entrance. Emerald Ridge Trail leads to a face-on view of Tahoma Glacier. The route gains 2,000 feet in 2½ miles. It goes through good goat country. The trailhead is 7½ miles north of Paradise Road. St. Andrews Park is an easy 3 miler that parallels the last 3 miles of West Side Road. Both hikes can be combined into a rugged 12-mile trip with a 3,000-foot change in elevation.

All these trails require maps, available at park ranger stations.

Mt. Rainier National Park has a back door. The northwest corner is not connected to the net of park roads but must be approached separately for its own charms. State 165 rambles through the old coal-mining towns of Wilkeson and Carbonado, closely following the Carbon River. Some miles outside the park, State 165 becomes a gravel road leading to Mowich Lake in the park. The branch Carbon River Road is paved all the way to its end at the park boundary.

Mowich Lake, popular with canoeists, is also the launch point for a pair of 3-mile hikes across gentle terrain. One trail leads to Spray Park, the other to Eunice Lake. There is a tents-only campground at Mowich. On the other fork, Ipsut Creek has R.V. spaces. From the end of Carbon River Road, the Carbon Glacier Trail is a fine day hike of 3 miles. The walk can be extended 2 miles to a vast meadow of wildflowers and then stretched another 2 miles to Mystic Lake. The total gain in elevation is 3,500 feet.

The climbers' Rainier. With nearly 50 square miles of glaciers, some of the fiercest mountain weather in the world, and plenty of gnarled rock faces, Rainier presents nearly every climbing challenge imaginable. It remains an enduring fascination for mountaineers from near and far, and has been a training ground for expeditions headed for peaks from Alaska to the Himalayas.

But Rainier also offers routes gentle enough that anyone with determination and sound health can climb to the summit under the supervision of the park-sanctioned guide service. Thousands do it every year on a 3-day outing (costing about $215) that combines a day's basic instruction with a 2-day ascent beginning from Paradise.

The outfitter rents ice axes, boots, crampons, and backpack (about $24 per day), but climbers must bring their own mountain clothing.

The guide service also offers ice- and rock-climbing courses. For reservations or information contact Rainier Mountaineering, Inc., Paradise, WA 98397.

Ski Touring on Rainier: Rainer Ski Touring, adjacent to the National Park Inn at Longmire (6 miles from the Nisqually entrance), is the hub of ski action. Rental equipment includes telemark gear. The center also provides trail maps, current conditions, touring suggestions, and avalanche and weather reports; call (206) 569-2283.

The Paradise Visitor Center, 18 miles from the Nisqually entrance, provides shelter, rest rooms, and a cafeteria.

Several facilities in Ashford, just outside the Nisqually entrance, offer packages for ski tourers.

None of the park's trails or routes are set with a tracking machine or groomed. But trailheads in the park are signed, and routes are sometimes flagged or indicated with painted metal markers.

Outside the Park

Near Mt. Rainier National Park and on the approaches to it are a wildlife park, a farm museum, state parks, wilderness areas, and one of Washington's finest ski areas.

Northwest Trek, a wildlife park, belongs to Tacoma's metropolitan park district. However, the 600-acre habitat lies in the Cascade foothills 17 miles south of Puyallup on State 161. From the perspective of visitors to Mt. Rainier, it is just off State 7 near Eatonville.

A forest-lined road leads into the park. In the core area a central building houses a restaurant, souvenir shop, and demonstration stage where attendants work with animals ranging from buffalo calves to ferrets. Within walking distance are many animal exhibits, including beavers building behind a glass-front dam and both tundra and timber wolves. Another area offers over 5 miles of nature trails. But the highlight for most visitors is a 45-minute narrated tram ride through a 435-acre free-roaming area housing large hoofed animals—moose, bison, bighorn sheep, pronghorn antelope, and caribou.

The park is open daily most of the year; there is an admission fee. Call (206) 832-6116 or write to the park at Eatonville, WA 98328 for complete information.

Pioneer Farm Museum is on Ohop Valley Road between State 7 and State 161 in Eatonville. Visitors are invited to join in such pioneer activities as milking the cows. The museum is open daily from June through Labor Day, weekends the rest of the year; call (206) 832-6300 for more information.

The Green River Gorge State Park Conservation Area protects a unique 12-mile corridor along the Green River north of Enumclaw. The state park area has three units: Nolte, with swimming and fishing in Deep Lake; Flaming Geyser, with old test holes drilled for coal and gas exploration; and Kanaskat-Palmer, with 50 campsites (19 hookups).

Federation Forest State Park preserves a virgin stand of timber on 619 acres along State 410 about halfway between Enumclaw and the northeast corner of Mt. Rainier National Park.

Poised on a bench above the White River, the park contains a striking range of plant-life communities, several of which can be seen on the 1.5 miles of interpretive trails. There is also an interpretive center in the park, as well as 9 more miles of hiking trails.

Crystal Mountain, most famous as a ski area, is in fact a year-round attraction for lovers of the outdoors.

In winter, the ski area runs three triple chair lifts and 6 double chairs. The great bowl has over 3,000 feet of vertical drop from a peak of 7,000 feet. Thirty-three miles of trails wind through lift-serviced and back-country acres. Lighted runs are available for night skiing.

In addition to its deep snow and varied runs, the area has a wider range of accommodations and after-ski activities than most other ski areas in Washington.

In summer, a chair lift hauls hikers up out of the bowl to a restaurant and trailheads for hikes ranging from easy to strenuous. Other trails depart from parking lots at or near the ski area. Crystal Mountain is also a launch point for the Pacific Crest Trail and other long hikes. (The trails quickly ease into Mt. Rainier National Park; back-country permits are required for overnighters.) Maps and descriptions of hikes in the area are available at the facilities at Crystal.

Tennis courts and rental horses are available. For more information, call (206) 663-2300.

The area is just off State 410, 76 miles from Seattle, about 2 miles short of the White River Entrance to Mt. Rainier National Park.

Another major ski area is only a few miles south and east of the park at White Pass (see page 80).

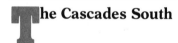he Cascades South

In spite of towering Mt. Adams and Mount St. Helens and in spite of craggy Goat Rocks Wilderness, the range south of Mt. Rainier is the gentlest part of the Cascades in Washington.

It is possible to make technically difficult rock and ice climbs here, but much of the region's attraction is more whimsical: huckleberry picking, mushroom hunting, and the like. Summer hiking is particularly agreeable, not only because there are many day hikes, but also because the weather tends to be warmer and drier than it is farther north. Not least, forest roads are plentiful, giving visitors better chances to drive close to a desired point than more rugged areas permit.

From an outdoorsman's point of view, to speak of the Cascade Mountains south of Mt. Rainier is to speak of Gifford Pinchot National Forest lands.

Within the forest are the two great peaks of the south state—Adams and St. Helens—as well as the White Pass Highway, major recreational waters of Packwood and Spirit lakes, and many other lakes and streams.

White Pass

The White Pass Highway, U.S. 12, connects Chehalis on Interstate 5 with the Central Washington city of Yakima. The link provides its users with some excellent mountain scenery, a clear image of the difference between wet west and dry east, and—as all the passes do—access to recreation in variety.

The logging town of Morton marks the beginning of mountainous country on the west side, but it is Packwood, near the summit, that serves as headquarters for hikers, campers, horsemen, fishermen, and boaters. Road-free Packwood Lake is a short hike away. White Pass Ski Area and its resort are but a few miles east. A sketchy summer-only, four-wheel-drive road ambles southward from Packwood along one edge of Goat Rocks Wilderness, a mecca for hikers and equestrians. This road continues: one branch leads west to the Lewis River reservoirs, another to Carson on the banks of the Columbia, and yet a third to White Salmon-Bingen, also on the Columbia. But it is not a recommended route.

Several National Forest Service roadside campgrounds are in the region. La Wis Wis (107 sites) is near the junction of U.S. 12 and State 123 east of Packwood. White Pass (20 sites) and Dog Lake (17 sites) are on U.S. 12 at White Pass. Several smaller campgrounds are tucked back along forest roads.

Packwood proper has motels and commercial trailer parks along with stores, gas, and other services. It also is the site of a National Forest Service ranger station.

Packwood Lake. A 17-site National Forest Service campground and a resort with rental boats sit near the outlet dam of the lake. The only access to the area is via a 4.3-mile hike from the end of Forest Road 1320. (Inquire at Packwood ranger station for road directions.) At a 2,867-foot elevation, the lake occupies a forested alpine basin looking straight up to Goat Rocks. The serenity of the place is at least as appreciable as the supply of trout.

West of the lake is a network of hiking and horseback trails. To the east is Goat Rocks Wilderness Area.

Goat Rocks Wilderness Area. Much of the 82,680-acre wilderness soars above the tree line, a constantly shifting mixture of alpine meadow and bare rock. Within the area's boundaries, 95 miles of hiking trails reach most of the alpine areas. Indeed, perimeter trails put nearly all within reach of day hikers as well as back-country campers. All but 10 miles of the trail system are open to horses in a region generally well developed for both pack trips and short trail rides. (As in all

---

The incomparable garden
At Crystal Mountain and all through the Cascade foothills, August wildflowers enchant everyone.

Hints for High Country Hikers

Wilderness hiking, as all veterans know, wants more skill than merely putting one foot in front of the other for the required distance.

At least half (and sometimes all) of the pleasure comes with being prepared to deal with uncertain weather and all the other whims of nature.

The U.S. Forest Service and the National Park Service offer the following advice to wilderness hikers, and especially to campers:

1. Do not travel alone. Recommended minimum party size is four.

2. Have proper equipment, to include:

- Sturdy boots with lug soles and ankle protection
- Loose-fitting, easy-on-easy-off clothing suitable for rain, wind, or cold
- Extra food and clothing
- Whistle (three blasts is the universal SOS)
- Map
- Compass
- Flashlight
- Fire starter (candle)
- First-aid kit
- Pocket knife
- Sunburn protection
- Waterproof matches

3. Plan your trip, tell family or friends of the plan, then follow it. (One experienced hiker says, "Tell everybody—hotel clerks, cab drivers, newspaper boys, maids, garage attendants, and anybody else you can find.") Vacationers, especially, need extra people aware of their plans. Checking in at a ranger station is the best bet of all.

4. Familiarize yourself with the trail and general area from a map and from any other sources. (The Mountaineers publish trail guides to all of mountainous Washington. These are widely available in bookstores and are quite reliable.)

5. Be in good physical condition. Do not over-extend yourself.

6. Be weather-wise. Both wetness and wind increase body heat loss.

7. Make camp (emergency or otherwise) before dark. Travel only in daylight hours.

Make camp near water, if possible. Water is more important than food. (Nowadays, most sources of drinking water carry nasty micro-organisms. It is generally wise to disinfect pond or stream water through 10 minutes' boiling, or with water purification tablets.)

Veteran backpackers know to carry everything they need into wilderness and other protected areas, where the only permitted use of resources is taking downed wood for fires. The trick is to limit pack weight to 35 pounds, maximum for comfortable uphill hiking.

Fire, not incidentally, requires careful use. The Forest Service recommends that hikers do not smoke on the trail, only during stops in safe places. Camp and cooking fires must be on bare earth and must be doused with water. (Burying live coals is risky; they may smoulder for hours, then break out anew.)

As courtesy to those who follow, all litter should be packed out.

Where trails are marked, it is in the interest of preserving delicate ecological communities to stay on them. Where trails switchback, shortcutting leads to erosion at least, and may cause rockfalls onto hikers below.

---

wilderness areas, riders here must carry feed for their stock.)

The season is short. Most trails open to foot traffic by mid-July, but snow can remain on higher trails—especially the Cascade Crest section of the Pacific Crest Trail—into August. Even in summer, foul weather can brew up quickly, so adequate gear is necessary.

Most perimeter trails reach in from the western boundary of the Wilderness Area. Forest roads running south from Packwood lead to the trail-heads. However, the Pacific Crest Trail, which crosses U.S. 12 at White Pass Campground, is hard to pick up anywhere but there. It runs 42½ miles

southward through the wilderness area without touching another road. (When it finally does, it only touches a forest road midway between the Goat Rocks and Mt. Adams wilderness areas.) Only five other trails intersect.

White Pass Ski Area. White pass has one of the most elaborate ski areas in the state—and some of the most elaborate accommodations to go with its runs. The vertical drop is 1,500 feet, from a top of 6,000 feet. Four double chair lifts, two pomas, and a rope tow serve the hill, which has a main bowl and several narrow runs cut through forests. Runs range from terrifying to bunny slope; the longest is 2 miles. The area also has a maintained 15-

kilometer cross-country track, as well as back-country routes in nearby Goat Rocks Wilderness.

The overnight lodge is supplemented by condominium rentals. Packwood to the west and Rimrock to the east are nearby sources of accommodations, and Yakima, 50 miles east, is also a base camp for White Pass skiers.

Rimrock Lake and Tieton River. U.S. 12 slips along one shore of Rimrock Lake, then stays with the Tieton River for mile after scenic mile on the route to Yakima. This is fishing country. Along the lake are commercial resorts, summer homes, marinas, public boat launches, and a campground (Indian Creek, with 45 sites).

East on the river come—in order, between mileposts 167 and 171—four National Forest Service campgrounds called Hause Creek (49 sites), River Bend (6), Wild Rose (11), and Willows (16). All adjoin a cold, clear stream limited to fly fishermen. These miles of alternating riffles and pools, with tree-lined banks and snowy mountains in the background, are the stuff of calendar photographs, to say nothing of joyous fishing for the pure sport of it.

Mount St. Helens

Until May 18, 1980, Mount St. Helens was, in its almost perfect symmetry, one of the most beautiful volcanic mountains in Washington, perhaps in the West. On that day a massive explosion blew the top 1,300 feet off the peak, gouging a deep crater. The blast leveled 230 square miles and killed 57 people.

The eruption was accompanied by far-ranging clouds of ash and steam, huge landslides, flooding, heavy ash deposits, and devastating mudflows that choked the Toutle River and buried Spirit Lake.

Since the 1980 eruption, the volcano has continued to vibrate with occasional tremors and to otherwise percolate, but throughout the devastated areas, regrowth has begun. Downed timber still floats on the remains of Spirit Lake.

St. Helens is now the center of a national volcanic monument. There is a restricted zone, but a new network of trails and rebuilt roads makes it possible to get good views of the volcano. Climbers may enter the restricted zone on Mount St. Helens under a special permit system.

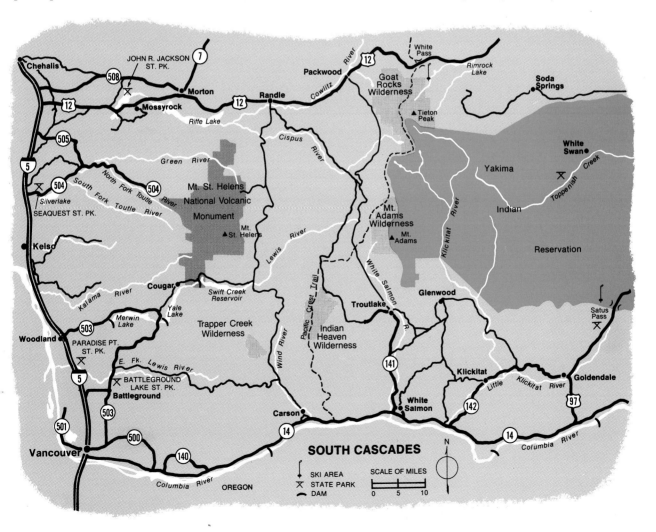

There are no campgrounds within the national monument, but several are located within driving distance.

The monument can be approached from the west, south, or east. To the west is the main visitor center, next to Silver Lake at Seaquest State Park. Take Exit 49 from I-5 near the town of Castle Rock; it's 5 miles to the visitor center.

The other access from the west is State 503 from Woodland. A bulletin board is located at Yale Lake, 1⅘ miles west of Cougar on State 503. At Pine Creek, 19 miles east of Cougar on a local road, an information center is open in the summer. Along this route are thousand-year-old lava tubes.

From the south, a local road—not all of it paved—leaves State 14 at Carson and joins the Cougar road.

Visitors approaching from U.S. 12 (north of the monument) can stop for information in the summer at Iron Creek, 8 miles south of Randle via a local road.

In the winter, cross-country skiers can follow a network of trails north of Cougar. A Snow Pass (available in town or from the Forest Service) is required for the Snow Park areas.

For maps and further information, write the visitor center at 3029 Spirit Lake Highway, Castle Rock, WA 98611; telephone (206) 274-4038.

The Columbia Side

Great, snowy Mt. Adams and some fine alpine meadowlands rise up from the banks of the Columbia, generously open to those who prefer to stay with the car, infinitely welcoming to hikers and backpackers.

Mt. Adams Wilderness Area. This roadless wilderness area encompasses the snowy peak and a considerable expanse of wooded flanks below.

The woodlands are notable for supporting an exceptional variety of trees, shrubs, and flowers. Here, all together, are species otherwise found on both sides of the Cascades and in the Rockies and Sierra Nevada.

The Pacific Crest Trail runs through the wilderness area, staying principally in meadowlands on the west side of the mountain. Three well-established routes to the summit are not difficult technical climbs, but they do require ice equipment and fair technique. The ascent takes about 10 hours.

Land of eternal snow

Camping in the snowy Cascades is high adventure in every sense. Strong updrafts produce lens-shaped cloud.

The Mt. Adams ranger station is at Trout Lake, the end of State 141 from White Salmon.

Several small National Forest Service campgrounds lie along forest roads just outside the wilderness area's southern boundary. The names are Morrison Creek (9 sites), Cold Springs (2 sites), and Timberline (3 sites).

Bird Creek Meadows. Once a part of Gifford Pinchot National Forest, Bird Creek Meadows on the southeastern flank of Mt. Adams reverted to the Yakima Indians a few years ago. The Yakimas have maintained the old campgrounds at Bench, Bird, and Mirror lakes, offering hiking, swimming, canoeing, and fishing on their lands for nominal overnight fees.

Both here and at Cold Creek, the mountain views are glorious, and the closer looks at meadows are full of the more intimate beauty of alpine wildflowers from July into September.

The road to the Bird Creek area begins at Trout Lake and runs 18 miles under National Forest Service numbers, all slow and hard to drive.

Wind River. From Carson, a side road pokes up into the Wind River drainage, one of the most fully developed hiking and camping districts in Gifford Pinchot National Forest.

In a tight cluster at Wind River are a ranger station, a nursery forest, an arboretum, and a trout hatchery. Campgrounds loosely ring this core area.

At Whiskey Creek, a branch road heads toward Goose Lake and Red Mountain lookout. From Red Mountain, a 1½-mile trail leads to the Indian Racetrack, a straight-line race course 10 feet wide and 1,000 feet long, in ancient times the testing ground of Indian horsemen of the region.

It is possible, although taxing, to continue eastward on forest roads to Trout Lake, or to push north into the Lewis River drainage (see page 68).

The Central Cascades

Two great passes—Snoqualmie and Stevens—open wide the central Cascades to human exploration.

Both routes—but especially Snoqualmie—have been developed by human hands into reliable all-year passes with no few creature comforts along the roadways. Aside from their businesslike function of getting people somewhere else, both highways run in close contact with outdoor recreation: summer hiking, camping, and fishing, and snow sports in winter.

Alpine Lakes Wilderness

As for backcountry, no great volcanic peaks punctuate the range at its midsection. Rather, a freak of geological chance created hundreds of lakes in a topsy-turvy terrain. These lakes range from tiny tarns well above the tree line to sizable reservoirs down in heavily wooded foothills. A great number of these lakes lie between the two passes in a region designated as a wilderness area. It is administered by both the Mt. Baker–Snoqualmie and the Wenatchee national forests.

Snoqualmie Pass

Low, wide Snoqualmie is Washington's best pass for people in a hurry, be they on business or in search of quick respite from urban cares. From Seattle all the way to Ellensburg, I-90 is four lanes. In winter, snowplows are almost as thick as passenger cars. Snow conditions at the pass are recorded; telephone (206) 455-7900.

For Seattleites, the countryside around the pass has become a sort of "woods at the edge of town." In summer, hikers flock to gentle, well-groomed trails and fishermen crowd well-stocked lakes and streams virtually at roadside. In winter, a row of pass-top resorts makes Snoqualmie the state's focal point for skiers.

Because the road is so reliable and the recreation so accessible, this is the best place for a visitor who has time for only a sampler of mountains. On the other hand, Snoqualmie is not Washington's most rewarding pass for autobound collectors of dramatic mountain scenery or picturesque villages. (Combined with Stevens as a day-long loop drive, though, it becomes the quick leg of a richer exploration.)

The towns. Beyond the urban sphere of Seattle, North Bend is the only highway town of any size west of the pass. In North Bend are a ranger station for Mt. Baker–Snoqualmie National Forest and a historical museum. Mount Si, the most climbed of Washington's peaks, looms just off the freeway next to town.

Near North Bend, just north of the freeway, is Snoqualmie Falls, a thundering cataract during the spring snowmelts. A short distance farther along the road, at the town of Snoqualmie, is a railroad museum with enough track to run short excursions of old steam trains; trips go as far as the depot in North Bend.

To the east, side-by-side Cle Elum and Roslyn are the only sizable towns near the freeway between the pass and Ellensburg.

Cle Elum has, as a particular point of interest, a telephone museum at 221 East First Street; here is housed the sort of gear otherwise found only in French hotels. Neighboring Roslyn has a museum of old coal mining equipment. Both museums are open afternoons during the summer, or by appointment.

Hiking and camping. Snoqualmie Pass Highway runs through gentle enough terrain to allow easy outdoor recreation along the highway or on spur roads leading away from it. Several large lakes adjoin the road; the wilderness Alpine Lakes hide away in hikers' country to the north.

Curiously, the big lakes are on the east side of the pass. Some westside hikes reach small lakes.

Denny Creek and Tinkham campgrounds, with about 40 units, flank the freeway just west of the pass. These National Forest Service developments are the head of a complex network of day-hike and longer trails. The longer routes lead into the Alpine Lakes Wilderness.

East of the summit, Keechelus, Kachess, and Cle Elum lakes parallel each other only a few miles apart. Keechelus, flanking I-90 to the south, is stocked with fish but otherwise not developed. Kachess is well developed as a lake for fishermen and boaters. A Forest Service road runs along the west shore of Kachess to a 178-site Forest Service campground and Box Canyon boat launch. Beyond this point, Little Kachess beckons paddleboaters with informal lakeside campsites, an annual restocking of trout, and an absolute absence of powerboats. Back on the opposite side of the highway, Lake Easton State Park has 145 campsites (45 hookups) on a small impoundment of water just below the main body of Lake Kachess. It also offers a boat launch, play area, and day-use picnic area. From I-90, Exit 63 leads to Kachess; Exit 70 runs into Lake Easton.

Cle Elum Lake has private resorts catering to fishermen. State 903 is the exit from I-90. The state road pushes along the eastern shore of the lake, continuing to a resort and campground at Salmon la Sac.

Iron Horse State Park extends 25 miles eastward along the I-90 corridor from the town of Easton. It features a nonmotorized recreational trail, the John Wayne Pioneer Trail. To reach the park and trail, take Exit 71 from I-90 at Easton or, in Cle Elum, park east of the old railway depot at the end of Seventh Street.

Although more access routes to Alpine Lakes are along U.S. 2, the Stevens Pass Highway, there are three routes from I-90—two easy, one tougher.

The Pratt Lake group can be reached from Denny Creek over a ranging net of trails.

A formal trail leads 4 miles from the Alpental Ski Area at the pass to Snow Lake, largest of several lakes in the Snow Lake group. Less formal trails lead to the others.

Ingalls Lake is the main event among day hikes in the region, especially during its show of fall color. A 3½-mile trail climbs 2,600 feet. The rewards for making the steep, rocky climb include a striking display of alpine opposites—jagged spires and gentle basins, snowfields and parklands, gnarled pines rooted in ice-polished granite slabs, and—in season—fat cutthroat trout in the depths of Ingalls and the golden light of Lyall's larch in fall dress.

To get to the Ingalls Lake trailhead, leave I-90 at Cle Elum (Exit 85) and drive 6 miles east on State 970 to Teanaway Road. Take this road north 23 miles, following signs to North Fork Teanaway at all junctions. The parking area is the trailhead. A trail map available at the ranger's office in North Bend is required.

Winter sports. Snoqualmie Pass—accessible and reliably snowy—was Washington's earliest developed ski area. It still has more groomed slopes than any other pass in the state. Once exclusively a day-use area, it has developed a substantial number of overnight accommodations, restaurants, and other amenities for those who would stay for a time.

Four ski areas form a tight cluster. Three of them (Alpental, Ski Acres, and Snoqualmie) are joined by a single lift-ticket system, shuttle bus service, and trails. A Snow Phone, (206) 236-1600, operates year-round with information on snow conditions and services.

Alpental's slopes range from 5,400 feet down to 3,200. They are served by four double chair lifts, a poma, and four rope tows. The area has several condominiums with rentals, a restaurant, and a bierstube.

Ski Acres has one triple chair lift, six double chair lifts, and six rope tows on its main slopes, which range in elevation from 3,900 feet to 2,900. Again, there is a condominium with rentals. The area also has a day lodge, cafeteria, bierstube, and lounge. Day care is available.

The Nordic Center at Ski Acres operates out of a separate log building. It offers lessons, rentals, and a network of set tracks, some lighted at night.

Snoqualmie's slopes, ranging from 3,900 feet down to 3,000, are served by two triple chair lifts, six double chairs, and seven rope tows. There's a restaurant at the top of the mountain as well as in the day lodge.

Pacific West, with slopes from 4,125 feet down to 2,800, has four double chair lifts and seven rope tows. It also has a cross-country area. Facilities include a condominium development, day lodge, bierstube, and nursery. For information, call (206) 633-2460.

Stevens Pass

Stevens Pass does not make much of a hole in the steep, high wall of the Cascades. Looking ahead, especially toward the great, rocky west wall, the pass promises little but a harrowing ride.

It is not so.

A rich recreational countryside spreads out on either side of the highway and on both sides of the pass. Fishermen haunt the roadside Skykomish and Wenatchee rivers and their tributaries for steelhead and trout. Campers and hikers come to this country in summer, followed by ski jumpers, downhill and cross-country skiers in winter. The mock-Bavarian village of Leavenworth is only the most advertised of several attractive towns.

As for the road itself, it once turned bus drivers' hair prematurely gray because it curled so tightly and so much. However, it always followed streambeds rather than hanging from cliffs. Now the route has been straightened and widened. In the steep stretches near the 4,061-foot pass, four-lane sections make the road fairly quick to drive even in snow season.

The Stevens Pass Highway, U.S. 2, cuts away from I-5 at Everett. It runs straight and fairly level through farm country all the way to the village of Startup, some 30 miles east. From there the terrain is earnestly mountainous across the pass to Leavenworth and beyond. Fall color and rushing water make Tumwater Canyon, above Leavenworth, the most scenic part of a scenic route.

Towns en route. As befits an old mountain pass, towns here come at closer intervals than modern freeway travelers have learned to expect. What is more, the mixture of farms in the lowlands and logging country up higher has yielded picturesque combinations. The three towns most likely to invite close inspection are Snohomish, Skykomish, and Leavenworth.

Snohomish, on fertile farmland, is an old-line dairy town. The original main street along the Skykomish riverfront has spruced itself up in recent years with restaurants and antique emporiums. Connoisseurs of Victorian architecture will find several admirable examples in the hilltop residential blocks across U.S. 2 from the riverfront area.

Fertile river bottom and dairy herds extend east beyond Monroe, almost to Sultan, where foothills finally crowd right up to the river bank. Beginning at Monroe, the Washington State Department of Fish and Game maintains public fishing accesses for winter steelheaders.

Skykomish, an old logging town, is so mountainous that the local school never has found a big enough flat spot to lay out a quarter-mile running track. (Fierce weather makes the track question moot but has helped the tiny high school produce several state champion basketball teams.) Closest westside town to the Stevens Pass ski area, Skykomish has a range of visitor facilities.

Leavenworth, over on the east slopes, remains the tourist capital of the Stevens Pass country despite challenges. Once dusty and forgotten after the loggers had come and gone, it has transformed itself into a prosperous Bavarian village.

The main street has blossomed with domes, cupolas, gingerbread balconies, and other bits of alpish architecture. The Chumstick Grange Hall has a half-timbered facade. Scroll-sawn eaves adorn the Forest Service ranger station. The phone company even calls itself *Telefonzentrale*.

Linguistic purists must forgive a good deal, but the atmosphere in bakeries, confectioners, souvenir shops, inns, and restaurants is *gemütlich*.

The Bavarian motif provides a festive backdrop for two well-attended festivals, celebrating autumn leaves and Christmas-tree lighting.

Not all is Germanic shops. Cross-country skiing is a major activity in the winter, with night-lighted tracks. In less snowy months, visitors can enjoy a handsome riverfront park just behind the main street. The town also supports the scenic but tough Leavenworth Golf Club, located on a hillside above the river, and plenty of nearby fishing and hiking. Accommodations (tending toward the quaint) are relatively abundant, and Wenatchee, 19 miles east, is a reliable source for more accommodations.

Hiking and camping. The available hiking and camping country in the region approaches an embarrassment of riches. The major areas are the Alpine Lakes on the west side and Wenatchee Lake on the east.

The Alpine Lakes area already has been noted in the section on Snoqualmie Pass, its other access. The following are day or weekend hikes, not outrageously strenuous.

Wallace Falls State Park. Between Snohomish and Skykomish, this park near Gold Bar is a good place to get out of the car and walk—to a thunderous 265-foot falls. To hike the whole distance takes 3 to 4 hours.

Dorothy Lakes group. This 9-mile trail touching four big subalpine lakes (Dorothy, Bear, Deer, and Snoqualmie) is especially popular with families. Leave U.S. 2 about 3 miles west of Skykomish at Miller River Road (watch for the Money Creek campground sign). Drive it south about 10 miles to the road end and trail number 1072. Island-dotted Lake Dorothy is only 1½ miles away. The trail continues to the other lakes.

Foss Lakes. A 6-mile trail passes five lakes. The first, Foss, is only 1½ miles distant. Fishermen's paths and cross-country routes lead to several other lakes at higher elevations. Leave U.S. 2 at the Foss River Road, about 2 miles east of Skykomish. Follow signs south about 6½ miles to the road end and West Fork Foss River Trail.

Lake Wenatchee. This popular lake is outside Alpine Lakes Wilderness by a whisker in ground distance, and by a larger margin because it is well developed for tourists. A fine fishing lake, it nestles into a basin that also attracts hikers, cross-country skiers, and snowshoers.

Lake Wenatchee State Park is at the lower tip, about 23 miles northwest of Leavenworth on a short local road off U.S. 2. Summer concessions include canoe and horse rentals.

Winter sports. Stevens Pass offers several winter sports areas.

The big groomed ski bowl right at the pass has 1,800 feet of vertical drop from a peak elevation of 5,800 feet. The bowl is served by 2 triple chair lifts and 6 double chairs. Facilities include a cafeteria and restaurant; a ski report hotline can be reached at (206) 634-1645. The area has no accommodations, but motels in Skykomish and Leavenworth are often used by skiers who stay in the region for more than a day.

Leavenworth Ski Bowl, with 500 feet of vertical drop, has two rope tows and cross-country ski tracks, as well as day lodge and lights for night skiing. The area is north of town; call (509) 548-7914. Leavenworth also has cross-country tracks in town.

The big lodge at Lake Wenatchee is the hub of a superior network of logging roads and trails. This is a popular spot in the Stevens Pass area for cross-country skiers and snowshoers because snow tends to be lighter and drier east of the pass than on the west, yet this area is not far past the summit.

In addition to these areas on the pass, one more, Mission Ridge, is within easy reach of U.S. 2 only 13 miles from Wenatchee on a local dead-end road. The area has four double chair lifts and two rope tows serving a bowl with 2,140 feet of vertical drop.

The North Cascades

The North Cascades are not the highest mountains in the world. They just look like contenders: craggy walls of granite looming nearly vertical for miles

Downhill skiers' delight
Snoqualmie and other Cascade passes have steep bowls for downhillers, gentler terrain for cross-country.

at a stretch, especially near the British Columbia border in the area called The Pickets.

In this forbidding terrain the sparse signs of civilization huddle along stream courses. Indeed, the first road across the north of the state opened only in 1972, a major feat of engineering even though the Skagit River on the west and Methow River on the east come very close together, providing natural routes for the highway for all but a few miles. State 20 will doubtless remain the only cross-state route in its part of the world.

For all the nearly impassable miles, the area is also a superior playground—a prime goal for fishermen, hikers, and campers, as well as high-country roamers and rock climbers. Theirs is a brief season, July through September in a typical year. Skiers, on the other hand, can start in November most years and finish on the Fourth of July if they don't mind a bit of slush under their skis. The Okanogan and Methow valleys give limitless chances to cross-country skiers and snowshoers.

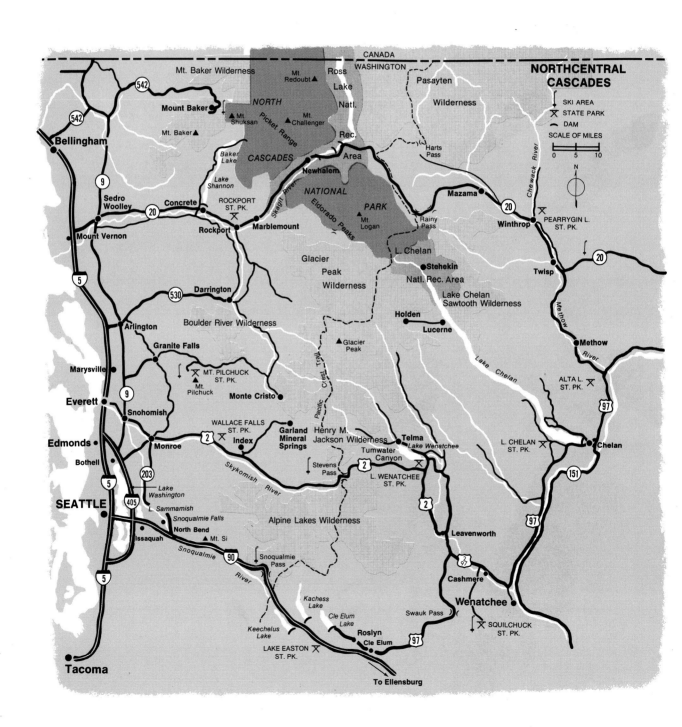

Generous parklands ease the path into the outdoors. The two almost untouched units of North Cascades National Park occupy the heights. Separating them—and forming a corridor for the North Cascades Highway—is Ross Lake National Recreation Area. Along the southern unit of the national park is Lake Chelan National Recreation Area. Glacier Peak Wilderness Area flanks Chelan to the west, covering parts of Mt. Baker–Snoqualmie and Wenatchee national forests. Pasayten Wilderness, administered by the Okanogan National Forest, hugs the British Columbia border east of the national park. These areas comprise almost 2,000 square miles, excluding other wilderness areas and national forest lands.

Unlike regions farther south, the east slopes here are richer recreational resources than are the west. Except for Mt. Baker and the lower tip of Ross Lake National Recreation Area, only a handful of westside parklands are available. The rest is either private land or too steep to cling to without climbing gear. Still, these westside parks are easily accessible from the Puget Sound basin, so they come first in this description.

Mt. Baker

There are two approaches to the Mt. Baker region—one from the north, the other from the south.

State 542 from Bellingham is the northerly route, running along the Nooksack River, then turning up to Mt. Baker Lodge and Ski Area. Near Maple Falls, Silver Lake County Park has camping and boating facilities, including boat rentals. The Glacier Public Service Center, 34 miles from Bellingham, is a joint operation of the U.S. Forest Service and the National Park Service. It provides maps, books, help in planning itineraries, and backcountry permits.

The southerly approach branches away from State 20, the North Cascades Highway, at the town of Concrete. From there, a local road pokes along one shore of Baker Lake. All these areas are within the Mt. Baker–Snoqualmie National Forest.

Mt. Baker Lodge, for day use only, is at Heather Meadows, an all-season anchor point. On summer weekends the double chair lift hauls people up to Panorama Dome for top-of-the-world looks at Baker and Shuksan. A road winds up from the lodge to 4,700-foot Austin Pass for those who would drive to their scenic highlight (and a 40-odd-site picnic ground). For hikers, several trails begin at or near the lodge.

In winter, Mt. Baker Ski Area serves skiers with six double chair lifts and four rope tows. The main bowl has 1,200 feet of vertical drop from a peak elevation of 5,540 feet. Located on a north

---

Paul Bunyan Games

Timber carnivals throughout the wooded Pacific Northwest bring the strong-man skills of the logger out of the forests and into town, where mere mortal folk can see how Paul Bunyan worked.

Some of these competitions are pure sport—ax throwing is a prime example. But most are workday skills honed to perfection. The sprint up and plunge back down a spar tree has its working counterpart. So does bucking, the cutting of a fallen tree into lengths, though the two-man saw widely known as a misery whip has long since disappeared from the commercial scene.

There is a professional circuit for which competitors have forsaken the working woods to chase big prize money and well-nigh unbelievable record times. Several of the major timber carnivals in Washington have both touring pro and local divisions, the latter for genuine loggers.

The following calendar lists durable timber carnivals with only approximate dates. Washington's Tourism Development Division publishes an annual calendar of special events with precise fair dates.

MAY

Mason County Forest Festival, Shelton, 5 days, midmonth.

JUNE

Deming Logging Show, Deming, 2nd weekend.
Timber Bowl Rodeo, Darrington, last weekend.

JULY

Loggerodeo, Sedro Woolley, 5 days, July 4 weekend.
Logging Show, Cathlamet, 3rd weekend.

AUGUST

Logger's Jubilee, Morton, 2nd weekend.

SEPTEMBER

Logger's Playday, Hoquiam, 2nd weekend.

---

slope, the area has Washington's longest season, traditionally finishing in July.

Baker Lake, on the south side of the mountain, has been developed for boaters, fishermen, campers, and hikers. Six boat launches dot the western shore. Five national forest campgrounds have about 80 tent and motor home sites.

In Cascades, alpine touches

The high Cascades are almost alpine in grandeur of scenery. In the foothill country, visitors find other notes reminiscent of the Alps. This hay field (above) for dairy cattle is near the town of Darrington. (The cattle are more likely to be Holsteins than Brown Swiss.) Leavenworth (right), on Stevens Pass Highway, has turned itself into a bit of Bavaria.

Stillaguamish River

Northeast of Everett, State 92 and a flurry of local roads poke into the Stillaguamish River basin. They lead, most particularly, to a pair of old mining towns. More rewardingly, they loop high enough to take in superior panoramas of snowy mountain peaks.

Although this is primarily conifer country, it yields massive autumn displays of golden alder, crimson vine maple, and the brown golds of big-leaf maple.

Informally known as the Monte Cristo back country, the area is well developed for camping, hiking, and stream fishing. Nearly all of 20 National Forest campgrounds border the Stillaguamish, the Sauk River, or tributary trout streams. Among them, the campgrounds have 94 tent sites and 123 R.V. sites. Gold Vasin is the largest unit, with 10 tent and 45 R.V. sites. Most are 5- to 10-site units.

The 85-mile Mountain Loop Highway—all two lanes, most of it paved and none of it difficult—allows an easy 1-day scenic drive. The southerly end of the route is at the town of Granite Falls, a few miles east of Everett and I-5. The north end is on I-5 at Exit 208. Along the way, the loop passes through the towns of Darrington and Arlington as well as Monte Cristo and Silverton. The former pair are alive and a-bustle; the latter two are mainly faded memories, but not quite ghost towns.

North Cascades Highway—Ross Lake

Heading east from the Puget Sound basin, State Route 20 waits a long time to turn into a mountain road. But when it finally leaves the farmlands of the Skagit River Valley and begins to climb through forest toward the tree line, it becomes memorable for some sudden, stunning looks at spires of rock, at fjordlike lakes, and, here and there, across alpine meadowlands. On the east side of Rainy Pass, the road slopes down into the Methow Valley, which looks as unlike the Skagit as any valley could. Few other roads in Washington point out quite so vividly the dramatic effect of the Cascades on regional climates, for few others connect valleys reaching so near each other from opposite sides of the range where it is so high.

This is the easiest route for hikers and campers to take into the heart of the North Cascades. Several fine trails start along the highway. Three fair-size developed campgrounds lie along the route. These attractions beckon motorists out of their cars without demanding long physical exertion. As a bonus, one of the campgrounds is on fishable, boatable Diablo Lake.

The highway has a limited season. Once the snows grow heavy in November and early December, the road closes down until the spring melt, possibly as late as April.

It is more accurate to say that only the high pass has a limited season. In fact, the western end of the road is popular in winter with Skagit River steelhead fishermen and eagle watchers. The stretch from Sedro Woolley up to Rockport attracts fisherfolk, including eagles. From Marblemount to Rockport the road passes through a 1,500-acre sanctuary for bald eagles, whose dwindling ranks do not look so thin here. Meanwhile, the eastern segment of the road carries a heavy traffic of skiers into the Methow Valley and Okanogan highlands.

Returning to the summer road, the following is a quick summary of its principal attractions.

Concrete is the last town of any size on the west side. After it, stores and service stations are few and far between until Winthrop, at the other end of the mountainous road. A National Forest Service ranger station is at Concrete, principally to serve the Baker Lake area (see page 89).

Rockport is a small vacation center. Rockport State Park has 62 campsites (50 R.V. hookups) in its 457 wooded acres. Alongside State 20 is a mile west of Rockport proper, the park gives access to a public fishing area between itself and Concrete, to Steelhead Park on the river bank at Rockport, and to a riverbank rest area just east of the town.

Marblemount, just outside Ross Lake National Recreation Area, has a National Park Service ranger station (source of back-country camping permits and information about canoe trips on Ross Lake), a gas station, and a store.

Between Marblemount and Newhalem is the Goodell Creek National Park Service Campground, a 20-site unit.

Newhalem is Seattle City Light's headquarters for the Diablo and Ross Lake power projects. A large picnic area nestles betwixt road and river, looking toward the powerhouse. This is the departure point for tours of Diablo Dam; these must be arranged in advance through Seattle City Light's main office (Skagit Tours Office, City Light Building, 1015 Third Avenue, Seattle 98104).

The tour takes in a powerhouse, an incline railway up to the dam, some antique generating equipment, and, not least, the awesome look from Diablo Lake Overlook up Thunder Creek to hanging glaciers on Colonial and Pyramid peaks.

A small resort is at the upper end of Diablo. It is a National Park Service concession and a mecca for trout fishermen. Reached by a spur road, this resort also is the gateway to Ross Lake.

Colonial Creek Campground flanks the Diablo shore on the lake's Thunder Creek arm, directly beneath the looming presence of Colonial Peak.

Freshwater Fishing

Lake and stream fishing in Washington does not seem to be as well known to outsiders as saltwater fishing for salmon, but it should be.

Steelhead is the prize catch of them all, but trout in variety may be had in every part of the state. In the regions east of the Cascade mountains, warm-water species—especially bass and crappie—are abundant. The Columbia River system supplements the list with shad and sturgeon.

A quick roster of freshwater fish includes the following:

Cutthroat. Also widely planted, the cutthroat is found more often in western than eastern Washington. Some Olympic Peninsula streams have sea-run populations much larger than those found in lakes. Though usually called a trout, it is a char.

Kokanee. A landlocked sockeye salmon, it is planted from hatcheries in many lowland lakes in western Washington and in some of the largest lakes of eastern Washington. The fish grows to several pounds but is prized more for its edibility than its ability to fight.

Smallmouth bass. The Snake River and the Columbia near its confluence with the Snake offer the most reliable fishing for this highly edible and hard-fighting species.

Steelhead. These are rainbow trout that spend part of each year in the sea, where abundant food allows them to grow to 20 pounds. They run in western Washington rivers for the most part, especially the Skagit and Skykomish on Puget Sound's east shore, and in most streams of the Olympic Peninsula. They also run in the Columbia as far up as a hatchery near Pasco.

It says something of the temperament of local fishermen that they prefer the winter run to the summer one, and do not think anyone is qualified to call themself a steelheader until he has watched ice form on his line.

Sturgeon. This fish, source of both caviar and delicious meat, ranges through the Columbia and Snake rivers. A big one weighs in at 1200 pounds (and cannot be kept).

Trout. Rainbow, eastern brook, and Dolly Varden all are available, especially in mountain lakes and streams. Generally, lakes are more productive than streams, though many heavily fished waters of both types are stocked annually. The Cascades are the focal point, but mountainous areas in both the northeast and southeast corners of the state have superior waters of their own.

Many Cascade streams are designated as "quality waters," which means they may be fished only with flies. The Washington Department of Game regulates freshwater fishing, and steelhead and cutthroat in salt water as well as fresh.

When, where, and whether you need a fishing license vary depending on how old you are and what you're fishing for. The regulations are complicated. Licenses are renewable on January 1, except for steelhead punch cards (which expire April 30).

Freshwater fishing licenses and steelhead punch cards are often sold at sporting goods shops and resorts.

Information about fishing areas and current regulations is available through the game department headquarters at 600 N. Capitol Way, Olympia, WA 98504; telephone (206) 753-5700.

A National Park Service campground, it has 149 campsites—some on each side of the road—a boat launch, showers, and other amenities. Several trails launch out from the area.

Ross Lake overlook adjoins the highway a few miles east of Colonial Creek. Once at the overlook, visitors have nothing to do but admire the view.

Only from Diablo Lake is Ross accessible. A boat travels from Diablo Dam to Ross Dam. The climb up from Diablo to Ross brings one to the floating resort on Ross. The narrow, 24-mile-long lake reaches north to the British Columbia border; it is a paradise for trout fishermen (the season opens late in June) and canoeists. Both make happy use of a rough dozen uplake boat-in camps.

Although the resort has rental boats, many canoeists bring their own. They paddle 3 miles up Diablo Gorge to the dam, having made advance arrangements through Ross Lake resort. The resort will ferry canoes up to Ross Lake on a stake-sided truck for a modest fee.

Diablo Lake Resort charges a parking fee and launch fee.

Ross and Diablo are both subject to sudden hard winds. Any newcomer who plans to canoe should seek advice and maps from the National Park Service ranger at Marblemount before setting out.

Not far beyond Ross Lake Overlook, the National Recreation Area boundary swings sharply northward, while State 20 continues its eastward way. This does not end the unspoiled scenery, however.

At Rainy Pass, the Pacific Crest National Scenic Trail crosses the highway. Terrain is tough both north and south. For those who would take a short stroll, a separate, gentle trail leads south from the pass 1.4 miles to Lake Ann.

Whistler Basin Viewpoint gives the road's closest view of a fragile alpine meadow. This one, like most, lights up with wildflowers in July or early August.

Washington Pass marks the beginning of a long, slow descent into the Methow Valley. Half a mile from the highway, a parking lot marks the beginning of an easy trail to an overlook that takes in Early Winters Creek, Snagtooth Ridge, Cooper Basin, Kangaroo Ridge, Liberty Bell Mountain, and more. Even a beat cop or a retired waiter would not resent the walk when sun shines on the view.

Early Winters, high up in the Methow Valley, marks the first return to civilization for eastbound motorists. An information office for the Okanogan National Forest is here, along with a six-unit tent campground. Between Washington Pass and Early Winters are two highwayside National Forest Service campgrounds, Lone Fir (26 sites) and Klipchuck (12 sites).

Harts Pass, at the end of a 23-mile road hewn out of rock in the 1880s for gold prospectors, is the northernmost road access in the U.S. to the Pacific Crest Trail.

A short but steep hike from Harts Pass campground along the crest trail to 7,300-foot Slate Peak rewards the hardy with a view even more grandiose than the one at Washington Pass overlook. This one reaches west to Mt. Baker and south to Glacier Peak. Just here, the trail touches the Pasayten Wilderness (see page 94). The road reaches up to Slate Peak, for those unable to walk it, but the flavor is not the same.

Heading south along the trail toward Rainy Pass and State 20 is a long walk with no nearby intermediate goals.

The road into Harts Pass will accommodate autos but not trailers. It branches away from State 20 at the Early Winters Information Station. Six small tents-only campgrounds line the way.

Winthrop was a town of sagging fortunes before the North Cascades Highway was completed. It has duded itself up with wooden sidewalks, false-front stores, and other good-as-the-movies westernisms as befits its new role as hub for travelers into the North Cascades National Park, the Pasayten Wilderness, and other parts of the Okanogan country.

The town is the commercial center of the Methow Valley, which in turn is a headquarters for pack-train operators during the summer and a haven for cross-country skiers and snowshoers in winter. Though not numerous, accommodations for travelers astonish with their diversity. The range is from modest hotel to refurbished stage-stop hotel to plush mountaintop lodge. The latter, Sun Mountain, caters particularly to cross-country skiers; it offers lessons and guided tours on 30 miles of maintained trails. Loners also are welcome on the trail system.

A National Forest Service ranger station is located in Winthrop.

Four miles east, on eastside Methow Road, is the North Cascades Smokejumper Base, home of an airborne firefighting unit responsible for five national forests. Time a visit right, and training jumps will end well within hollering distance. The base is open daily during daylight hours.

Lake Chelan National Recreation Area

Lake Chelan cuts a long, deep slice into the eastern flank of the Cascades. At the head of the lake, far into the mountains and far beyond the last road to the outside, is the largest single development of the North Cascades National Park.

The old campers' and hikers' village of Stehekin was a base for forays into the Cascades long before the park was established. Now, as a park concession, three old resorts have been consolidated into one, North Cascades Lodge, which has both two-story alpine lodge buildings and separate cabin units.

A daily boat makes the 110-mile round trip between Chelan (see page 108) and Stehekin. A remarkable transition takes place along the way. At Chelan, low, lion-hide hills rim the lake, giving no hint that the terrain on either side of this mile-wide, 1,500-foot-deep souvenir of a glacier quickly will turn to high, steep, forested slopes.

Visitors can fly in as an alternative to the boat. At the slower end of the scale, the willing can walk the last 6 miles from Moore to Stehekin.

Some visitors come to fish, mostly in deep trout holes along the Stehekin River. Some come just to relax. Most come to hike or set out on horseback for pack trips.

A 23-mile-long dirt road ambles yet deeper into the heart of the North Cascades from Stehekin. The lodge runs a shuttle bus along the road and rents cars.

Ten day hikes begin at Stehekin or along the road, as do eight well-maintained loops requiring 2 to 4 days. Finally, cross-Cascade hikes can begin or end in the region.

A local concessionaire runs the pack trips. The firm has an established, summer-only schedule for these. The lodge remains open the year around.

Detailed information is available from the Chelan Chamber of Commerce, the North Cascades National Park office at Chelan, and the National Forest Service ranger station at Chelan.

Glacier Peak Wilderness

Glacier Peak is the ridgepole of the Cascades between Lake Chelan to the east and the Suiattle

River drainage above Darrington to the west.

It is purely the preserve of hikers and equestrians. No road pokes into it. Few day hikes reach inside its remote borders, although access roads come to its edges along the Suiattle River on the west and at Holden and Stehekin on the east. Holden is a religious retreat; a road leads to it from the Lake Chelan shore at Lucerne. Hikers are welcome to pass through.

Trails from these and a handful of other points reach up to join the Pacific Crest Trail, which winds through the wilderness.

Glacier Peak itself is a popular climb, not technically difficult by mountaineer's standards, but requiring first-rate equipment and reasonable technique on both rock and ice. The peak's elevation is 10,451 feet.

The season, predictably, is short. Passes along the trails open late in July or early August, then close again with the first heavy snows of October.

Pasayten Wilderness

Friendly as wildernesses go—because of both its gentle districts and its comparatively long season—the Pasayten Wilderness adjoins Ross Lake National Recreation Area on its east side, extending east into the Okanogan country from there. On the north it abuts British Columbia.

With the coming of the North Cascades Highway, several access routes became relatively easy. One is at Harts Pass, via a branch road from the highway at Early Winters (see page 93). Two more roads run north from Winthrop to the wilderness boundary, some miles east of Harts Pass but still in high country.

However, it is the Horseshoe Basin country in the Pasayten's northeast corner that is distinct for offering both gentler weather and gentler terrain.

By late June the relatively light local snowpack has melted away under an early sun. Snow-free routes run all the way to 8,000 feet.

The vast meadow of Horseshoe Basin is a superb example of what the Pasayten offers: miles of rolling tundra pocked with ponds and brooks, wildflower swales, groves of dwarf fir and whitebark pine, and a circle of rounded mountains that invite cross-country exploring.

To get to Horseshoe Basin, leave U.S. 97 at Tonasket, cross the Okanogan River, and follow signs 17 miles north and west to Loomis. Continue north 2 miles, then turn left on Forest Road 390. Follow this road 14 miles to its junction with a secondary road signed Iron Gate. Follow this very rough track about 5 miles to a parking area.

This territory is as popular with equestrians as with hikers. Pack-train operators are in both the Methow and Okanogan Valleys. The Forest Service can provide lists.

Useful Addresses in the Cascades

- Mt. Rainier National Park
  Longmire, WA 98397
- Mount St. Helens Volcanic National Monument
  Visitor Information
  3029 Spirit Lake Highway
  Cougar Rock, WA 98611
- North Cascades National Park
  Sedro Woolley, WA 98284
- Mt. Baker-Snoqualmie National Forest
  915-2nd Ave.
  Seattle, WA 98104
- Okanogan National Forest
  P.O. Box 950
  Okanogan, WA 98840
- Gifford Pinchot National Forest
  500 W. 12th Street
  Vancouver, WA 98660
- Wenatchee National Forest
  P.O. Box 811
  Wenatchee, WA 98801

Chambers of Commerce

- P.O. Box 43, Cle Elum, WA 98922
- P.O. Box 306, Darrington, WA 98241
- P.O. Box 845, Eatonville, WA 98328
- 436 N. Sprague St.,
  Ellensburg, WA 98926
- 226-8th St.,
  Leavenworth, WA 98826
- P.O. Box 38, Monroe, WA 98272
- P.O. Box 10, Morton, WA 98356
- P.O. Box 357, North Bend, WA 98045
- P.O. Box 402, Winthrop, WA 98862

Where the Cascades meet the Columbia

From the Oregon side, looking across Crown Point, Beacon Rock is dim in the mists upstream (below). Once at Beacon Rock, hikers in the state park begin one trail 600 feet above the river and almost straight above the shore. They finish (left) 4 miles upstream and far back from the river's edge.

In its powerful drive to the
sea, the Columbia carved
its own greatest monument

Columbia

The Columbia River Gorge contains some of the great dramatic scenery in North America, yet manages to be memorable for manmade details as much as for its natural grandeur.

The gorge is a river-cut gap through the Cascade Mountain Range. Its scenic high point comes in the heart of the granite mountains near Bonneville Dam, where the north bank rises steadily toward snowy Mt. Adams while, on the Oregon side, Mt. Hood looms close, in clear view. Beyond the Cascades, the walls of the gorge are steep basalt cliffs as far as the mouth of the John Day River.

In 1986 a Columbia River Gorge bill limited commercial and industrial development along 45 miles of river shoreline. The total area protected under the bill is 250,000 acres in Washington and Oregon.

Unlike most vastnesses, which discourage use, the Columbia has been a scene of hectic commerce from earliest Indian history to the present. This is because its course through the gorge to the sea offers the most reliable year-round route between coastal ports and interior farms for both Washington and Oregon. As such, it is one of those rare boundaries that unifies more than it divides.

Unable to change the gorge much, humans have instead changed the river that quarried it. Four great hydroelectric dams slow the water's rush, making the Columbia much less apt to flood.

The Columbia drops 200 feet in the 143 nautical miles from Pasco to Portland. In its free-running days, Cascade and Celilo falls and a few other spots gave riverboaters more drama than they wanted. Locks and canals softened the falls around the turn of the century.

Between 1938 and 1955, dams drowned first one and then another of the old falls and rapids. Some parts of the old locks remain in view at Cascade, but all the other rough spots hide beneath deep, slow water; the Columbia up to Pasco is a safe route for commercial barges and pleasure boats.

Up on the banks, trucks and railroads augment the barge traffic and every kind of car and camper supplements pleasure boats.

It is no trick at all to wake up in the wet, woodsy world of Paul Bunyan and drive into hot, dry, sparsely settled cowboy country in time for lunch.

A great many people from the west side of the Cascades drive the gorge as a loop trip to cure the inner city blahs. No few continue east to frolic in sun-warmed water at the Tri-Cities of Pasco, Kennewick, and Richland. Some who have come to fish the river have never gone back home.

Weather. Nothing points out the corridor quality of the Columbia between Portland-Vancouver and the Tri-Cities so well as the weather.

At the Paul Bunyan end of the gorge, Vancouver collects 39 inches of rain a year. The average temperature in July is 67°F., in January 38°F. Up in cowboy country in Richland, the annual rainfall is 7.5 inches, the average July temperature 75°F., and the average January reading 32°F.

But averages take the sting out. Vancouver sees the thermometer at 90°F or more on six summer days a year, while Richlanders see it at that level on 61 days.

Without mountains to cloud the issue, the progression from coastal maritime toward continental climate patterns is easy to see in changing vegetation with each passing mile, and likely to be felt.

Highways. On the Washington side, State 14 is it from Vancouver to Plymouth, where I-82 bends inland to shorten the trip to Kennewick. Except for a brief four-lane stretch from Vancouver through Washougal, State 14 is two lanes of asphalt. As far east as Bingen the going can be slow on hilly curves and through towns. East of Bingen the road becomes essentially level and straight, as fast as Interstate 84, the freeway over on the Oregon side.

For those who need to swap sides, opportunity knocks often. There are bridges at Vancouver; just upstream from Bonneville Dam; at Bingen-Hood River; a short distance downstream from The Dalles Dam; just downstream from John Day Dam; and at Plymouth-Umatilla. Between John Day Dam and Umatilla, a barge ferry connects Roosevelt on the Washington side with Arlington on the Oregon.

See additional maps on pages 100 and 101.

River Gorge

For those who would stay with the cooling river after I-82 turns across country, the bridge from Plymouth to Umatilla leads to U.S. 730/12, which passes some fine scenery en route to Pasco.

Boating. For anybody with a boat, the river itself is an alternative highway. Each of the four dams has a free lock, so boaters can run all the way from the river mouth at Ilwaco to Tri-Cities without leaving the water. Shoreside facilities and accommodations are plentiful all along the river.

Because of commercial navigation, traffic on the river stays tidy under Coast Guard control. Channels are marked clearly by buoys. On the odd occasion when wind roughens the waters too much, storm flags fly.

Bonneville Dam–the Granite Gorge

Eight miles east of Washougal, State 14 winds around the river side of a huge rock called Cape Horn. Here, hundreds of feet above the river, a three-car pullout offers an incomparable perspective on the granite gorge.

Almost straight down is an audaciously small farm, the scale-setter in the scene. Upstream, Beacon Rock, an even larger monolith than Cape Horn, reaching 848 feet above the river bank, hides Bonneville Dam behind it and still looks small in the panorama unfolding hill after hill to the east.

This is the heart—the part that keeps being re-elected a great scenic treasure.

Beacon Rock State Park encompasses the rock and a long piece of the gorge's wall. Nobody climbed the rock until 1901. Now ramps, steps, and switchbacks make the climb possible for any healthy soul who would gaze 10 miles downstream, farther upriver, or a few hundred feet across to the near wall of the gorge.

Straight across from the monolithic chunk of basalt, about 50 campsites and several picnic sites are the anchor points for a network of trails along the gorge wall. As summer warms, a swimming beach alongside Beacon Rock becomes a major park attraction.

Bonneville Dam, first dam built on the navigable Columbia (in 1938), offers a close-up look at its locks from the Washington side. In the main, though, it is oriented toward the Oregon shore, where there is access to an elaborate visitor center, a trout and sturgeon hatchery, an underwater fish-viewing station, and the powerhouse.

Four miles upstream, the toll "Bridge of the Gods" permits a quick change to the Oregon side.

Stevenson, a mile east of the bridge, has much of the air of a Mark Twain river town. Tugs moor here. The river bank has a scattering of local boats, some functional, some sinking, some sunk. In summer, back streets are full of kids dressed for a remake of Huckleberry Finn.

A sternwheeler conveys visitors on two-hour narrated tours between Stevenson and the Bonneville Dam Visitor Center. Passengers learn about local Indian legends, history, and geology.

Stevenson has been a logging town as well as a river port. A few miles upstream, near Underwood, is a genuine log flume—the most easterly one along the river. To learn more about local history, visit the Skamania County museum on Vancouver Avenue in the courthouse annex. In the museum, appropriately, are models of early steamships.

Carson is the turnoff point for a partially paved road leading north to Mount St. Helens National Volcanic Monument. It is also the home of a nursery and an arboretum with trails and informational signs. To reach the nursery, drive 9 miles north on Wind River Highway, then 1 mile west on Hemlock Road.

Bingen, 25 miles upstream from Stevenson, has a main street and principal buildings laid out to frame the Columbia just as roads and buildings frame the Rhine in the original Bingen in Germany. And at the west end of town a small winery draws its grapes from three local vineyards steep enough to satisfy any Rhinelander. Bingen Wine Cellars and its tasting room are housed in a big,

Germanically ornamented building full of shops.

Windsurfers flock to Home Valley Park to skim across the Columbia to Oregon's Hood River.

Roads here and just to the west make Bingen and neighboring White Salmon gateways into Gifford Pinchot National Forest and onto Mt. Adams.

The Basalt Gorge to McNary Dam

Bingen is at the edge of the forests and at the end of the granite gorge. Very quickly to the east come basalt cliffs at the river's edge, with rolling grasslands above them.

For a few eastward miles roadside points of interest come close-packed; then they grow increasingly sparse. No accommodations and few eating places are to be found on State 14 between Bingen and the Tri-Cities. The Oregon side compensates, especially at The Dalles, Boardman, and Umatilla.

The Dalles Dam, some 17 miles upstream from Bingen, comes first in a line of roadside attractions. It is the only one of the lower Columbia's four great dams that visitors can use to cross from one state to the other. The sturdy may walk, but a free train carts most visitors from the locks on the Washington side to the powerhouse, then to the fish ladder on the Oregon side, and back. A picnic park is on the Oregon side.

U.S. 197 bridges the river just downstream for those who need to swap sides with a car.

Horsethief Lake State Park is just above the dam. The distinctive feature of this 338-acre riverside park is an Indian petroglyph incised into basalt, but Horsethief is popular for camping (12 sites), picnicking (open and sheltered tables), swimming, and fishing. It has a boat launching ramp and a moorage.

Maryhill Museum, 18 miles above Horsethief, changes the pace entirely. On a high cliff overlooking the river, the building is a middle-of-nowhere Flemish-style manor house built in the 1920s by a Seattle lawyer named Sam Hill. Originally meant to be a residence, it was never lived in. Instead, Hill and friends slowly filled it with an odd gamut of fine materials: impressionist art (Manet, Cezanne, and others), Rodin sculptures, white elephants from the closets of Queen Marie of Rumania and Marshal Joffre of France, Indian artifacts from near and far, chess sets, amphorae. Maryhill is operated as a trust; there is a small admission fee.

Incidentally, weather governed the location of all of this. In the midst of a Seattle rainy spell, Hill decided that wet and dry must meet somewhere.

He sent someone out to find that spot; Maryhill was the choice.

Not far east of the museum is another of Hill's whimsical contributions to mid-Columbian culture, a concrete model of Stonehenge. Hill meant it to be a replica of the original in Great Britain, but he was four decades ahead of the decoding of that great Druid astronomers' measuring device, so the one on the Columbia points nowhere in particular. Signs on State 14 lead to the model.

U.S. 97 crosses State 14 two miles east of Maryhill. It bridges the Columbia some hundreds of feet below the intersection. Just upstream of the bridge is 98-acre Maryhill State Park. Once a Corps of Engineers park, it has 50 hookups, a boat launch and moorage, swimming beaches, and riverbank fishing spots.

Goldendale, north along U.S. 97, is the home of the Klickitat County Historical Museum (127 West Broadway, in a 1902 house) and Goldendale Observatory State Park. Here on a wooded hilltop one mile north of town is situated the nation's largest public telescope. Tours, exhibits, lectures, and telescope viewing are offered. Call (509) 773-3141 for hours, or write 1602 Observatory Drive, Goldendale, WA 98620.

About 15 miles further north along U.S. 97, Brooks Memorial State Park has 45 campsites (23 hookups), 40 picnic sites, and 9 miles of hiking through Ponderosa pine. Beavers are often seen here along the Klickitat River.

John Day Dam, not far upstream, is the least visitable of the four great dams, but visitors can watch its locks in operation from the Washington side.

From this dam eastward, the amusements on Washington's bank come seldom.

At Roosevelt, some 30 miles upstream, a toll ferry crosses the Columbia. The Roosevelt-Arlington ferry offers the only opportunity to get a car across the river between U.S. 97 and Umatilla.

This and a ferry from Puget Island to Westport, Oregon, are the last two on the big Columbia. The 12-car tug-and-barge ferry runs on call from 7 A.M. to 10 P.M. Citizens' band radios on each shore put would-be passengers in touch with the skipper. The ride covers 5.5 miles.

Crow Butte State Park is nestled in a quiet eddy of the river about midway between John Day and McNary dams. It has a fine sheltered swimming

---

The source of energy
Bonneville was the first great hydroelectric dam on the lower Columbia. It now has three bigger brothers generating electricity.

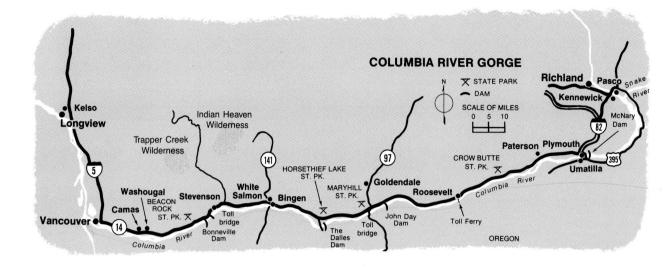

beach in shoal water, a boat launch, 50 hookups, and picnic sites.

River Ridge Winery. Above ground, the Paterson facility of Chateau Ste. Michelle, the state's largest wine producer, simulates a French manor; below ground are acres of production capability. Two thousand acres of vineyard slope down to the Columbia. Manicured lawns, a sun-capturing stone courtyard, and an interior hung with French tapestries and furnished with carved antiques add to the Gallic atmosphere. Guided tours end at a tasting room.

At Plymouth, a large municipal park comes in several sections. The major segment, on the riverbank, has campsites, a boat launch, and swimming.

McNary Dam is the farthest upstream of the dams on the navigable Columbia. Its locks, on the Washington side, have the highest lift of them all, 75 feet. Next to the locks on one side are a boat ramp and public dock, on the other a fish ladder and counting station.

Here State 14 connects with Interstate 82, which swings up to the Tri-Cities.

The Water-Cooled Tri-Cities

The Tri-Cities—Pasco, Kennewick, and Richland— have become a major weekend destination for sun-seekers from west of the Cascades. Though almost no water falls from summer skies, dams and rivers provide so much of it underfoot that this sunny region ranks second only to Puget Sound as an aquatic playground.

The Snake joins the Columbia here. Riverbank parks flourish in profusion on both streams, beck-

oning swimmers, water-skiers, fishermen, and just plain float-around boaters. The high season runs from May through October, but fine weather may come earlier and stay later.

Although golf and tennis are not so highly developed as waterborne recreation, both can be pursued with pleasure through a long season. Golf courses, in fact, stay open the year around.

Wineries in town and nearby are available for tours and tasting.

Those who insist on serious contemplation can come here to ponder energy. The combination of running water and cloudless skies has made this area a center of hydroelectric power generation. The U.S. Department of Energy's Hanford Site adds nuclear energy to the mix.

Richland grew out of Hanford, a closed government town built in the 1940s to nourish the Atomic Energy Works. Its rootlessness allowed it to become an uninhibited sprawl of contemporary shopping centers, motel rows, and residential neighborhoods.

Kennewick, its neighbor on the Columbia's west bank, connected by 7 miles of busy freeway, is a quiet retail and residential community and the pleasure boat capital of the region.

Pasco, across the Columbia from Kennewick, was settled in 1884. About half the size of the other two towns, it is a seat of agricultural industry, a major railyard, and the upper terminus of commercial barge traffic on the river.

Accommodations. All three of the cities have motels. Richland's are mostly on George Washington Way, which parallels the Columbia. Pasco's cluster near the airport.

Attractions. Highlights around the Tri-Cities range from the latest in high technology to down-to-earth agriculture.

• *Power.* The abundant river water and the presence of the Hanford Atomic Energy Works have made this region a veritable laboratory of energy.

Hanford Science Center, in Richland's Federal Building just off George Washington Way at Newton Street, is a complete museum-cum-learning center about all forms of energy, especially nuclear. Visitors can manipulate slave arms used for handling shielded radioactive materials as well as get answers to all manner of serious questions from oft-changed displays and knowledgeable staff.

For another view of energy, stop at the Fast Flux Test Facility visitor center, 13 miles north of Richland on the Hanford site. Here models describe the sodium-cooled nuclear reactor designed to test fuels and materials. For hours and directions, call (509) 376-5101.

Hydroelectric power is the main attraction on dam tours. There is a tour of the facilities at McNary, 25 miles down the Columbia (see facing page). In addition there are tours at Wanapum Dam, 60 miles up the Columbia via State 240, the Vernita bridge, and State 243; at Ice Harbor Dam on the Snake, 12 miles east via State 124; and at Lower Monumental Dam, 60 miles east on the Snake near Kahlotus, enroute to Colfax and the Palouse country. All explain the generation of hydroelectric power.

• *Wineries.* A brochure available from the Tri-Cities Visitor & Convention Bureau lists the many wineries in the area, with descriptions of facilities, directions, and visiting hours. Some are right in town, many are along U.S. 12 on the way to Yakima, and others are scattered to the east and south. Almost all offer tasting; Preston is the closest to town with a complete tour.

• *Other attractions.* Long before any of the energy sources came to be tapped, this was rich agricultural country. Irrigation has made it still richer. Any drive east toward Dayton or Walla Walla gets into the heart of the farm country.

Tomlinson's Dairy, on the Kahlotus Highway east of Pasco, shows dairying at its scientific best. Free self-guided tours include both the milking parlor and a calf nursery. The dairy is open daily.

In Pasco itself, a farmer's market in an open-air arcade brings home-pickled asparagus and fresh bread to town dwellers.

Railroad buffs can visit Burlington Northern's computerized rail switching yard 3 miles south of Pasco off U.S. 12 via Oregon Street. Call ahead, (509) 547-6246.

In the town of Pasco, the Franklin County Historical Museum at 305 N. Fourth Street is open in the afternoons, Wednesday through Saturday.

Parks and recreation. To experience the desert in the Evergreen State, visit the Juniper Dunes Wilderness, 8 miles northeast of Pasco off U.S. 395 on Phend Road at Juniper Forest Road. You can walk (not drive) through more than 7,000 acres of sand dunes and juniper groves, among wildflowers and desert wildlife—including many hawks.

Waterside parks fan out in every direction from downtown Kennewick, where Columbia Park serves as an admirable base point and/or measuring stick for all the rest.

Columbia Park, 434 acres strung out along 4½ miles of river bank, has a swimming lagoon at its south end, almost under the bridge carrying U.S. 12. At the north end is a concessionaire campground. In between are a short golf course, an island with a marina, several batches of kids' playground equipment, and a vast collection of picnic tables under mature shade trees.

Howard Amon Park in Richland is a smaller echo of Columbia for picnickers. It lacks a swimming area but does have boat launching ramps.

Two Rivers Park, 5 miles southeast of Kennewick and directly across the Columbia from the mouth of the Snake, is a 7-acre picnic and swimming park with a boat launch.

Hover Park, another 6 miles downriver, is 326 undeveloped acres for those who would fish or picnic in natural surroundings.

Two miles south of Pasco via U.S. 12, Sacajawea State Park occupies the tip of land where the Snake's north bank meets the east side of the Columbia. Ample picnic and play lawns roll gently under shading trees to a fine swimming beach, sheltered from boats by fences and patrolled by lifeguards. A boat moorage along the Snake side of the park caters to water-skiers.

Lewis and Clark camped on the spot in 1805; the park name commemorates their Indian guide.

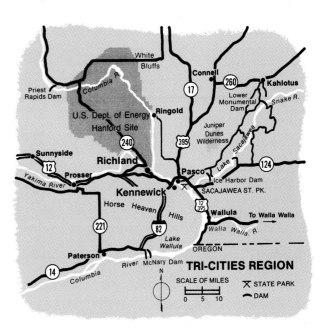

TRI-CITIES REGION

An interpretive center, open in the summer, provides explanatory material both about the expedition and about Indians.

A whole series of Corps of Engineers public parks dots the banks of the Snake. The first of them, going upstream, is Hood. On the south bank just upstream from U.S. 12 as it bridges the Snake, the picnic, swimming, and boating park is well shaded by mature trees. It has 60 campsites and 18 hookups.

Charbonneau is next on the south bank, 16 miles east of Pasco. Young, quite open until its trees grow, it has 20 campsites next to its swimming beach and boat launch. (Charbonneau, incidentally, was Sacajawea's husband. His first name was Toussaint.)

Fishhook, 27 miles east of Pasco via State 124, then 4 miles north on a spur road, is much like Charbonneau except that the campground accommodates 100.

Over the north bank is Levey Park, 14 miles east of Pasco via a county road along the river. Like the others it has fishing, swimming, a boat ramp, and camping (20 sites).

All of these are popular destinations for boaters from the Tri-Cities as well as land travelers.

For those who come without a boat, a large marina on manmade Clover Island at Kennewick has a variety of rentals, but especially rigs for waterskiers. Also on Clover Island are cruise boats, available either for scheduled tours or as charters.

● *Fishing* from boat or bank is diverse in these waters. In broad outline, steelheaders work the banks north of Pasco near a hatchery at Ringgold; bass fishermen stay along the riprap on the Pasco side of the river opposite Columbia Park; and sturgeoners head up the Snake looking for deep pockets. Fishermen after salmon and catfish distribute themselves widely.

● *Golf.* Six courses are open to public play within the three municipalities.

In Pasco, the well-groomed Pasco Municipal (18 holes; 6,524 yards; par 72) rolls steadily among loose plantings of mature trees, with just enough bunkers to keep a long hitter honest. It flanks U.S. 12 just north of town.

In Richland just off U.S. 12, the ambitiously designed Meadow Springs (18 holes; 6,980 yards from the back tees; par 72) flows through a small valley developed for homesites. In its youth it is open, but new trees are growing. Public play is limited, but visitors can frequently get a starting time. Richland Elks Golf Course (18 holes; 6,000 yards; par 69), just off State 224 in West Richland, is level and generally open but has some hazards. Sham-Na-Pum (18 holes; 6,458 yards; par 72) plays flat all the way and is quite open on the back nine. It adjoins George Washington Way on the south side of town.

In Kennewick, Tri-City Country Club (18 holes; 4,656 yards; par 65) is scenic and every bit as gentle as par promises. The course is on Underwood (State 14) west of downtown. Finally, Columbia Park Golf Course (18 holes; 3,100 yards; par 56) is dead level and wide open, a fine course for kids to get started on or for all hands on hot days when quicker is better. In Columbia Park, it is just far enough from the river bank to keep balls out of the water.

● *Tennis.* The Tri-Cities area was a hotbed of tennis long before the boom. The following public courts all have good surfaces and may produce a pickup game for a solo traveler.

In Richland, Howard Amon Park has four courts on Lee Street just off George Washington Way. Two are somewhat lighted.

In Pasco, Sylvester Park has four courts (three lighted) at Fifth and Sylvester. Not far away in Volunteer Park are another three courts. Volunteer is on Fourth (U.S. 395-Business) across from City Hall.

Richland, Pasco, and Kennewick high schools and Columbia Basin College add another 25 courts among them, all available when school is not in session.

Tri-City Court Club, with six indoor and four outdoor courts, allows visitors to play for hourly fees on a limited basis. The club is on the north side of Kennewick, near Richland's Columbia Shopping Center.

Amid the burning sands

At Tri-Cities, on the edge of a true desert, dams have made a vast watery playground rivaling Puget Sound.

Useful Addresses along the Columbia River Gorge

● Camas-Washougal Chamber of Commerce
P.O. Box 915
Camas, WA 98607

● Mid-Columbia Visitors Council
Port-Marina Park
Hood River, OR 97031

● Tri-Cities Visitor & Convention Bureau
P.O. Box 2241
Tri-Cities, WA 99302

A wide land that dams built,
this is home to the state's
cowboys, Indians . . . and farmers

Central

Grand Coulee Dam, along with Hoover on the Colorado River, is the granddaddy of giant hydroelectric dams in the West. On that count alone, it ranks year in and year out as Central Washington's premier visitor attraction.

However, having spawned many other hydroelectric and irrigation dams, Grand Coulee has also done much to turn Central Washington—the once inhospitable Columbia River Basin—into a summertime recreation ground in all the places where water has slowed and gathered.

"Basin" is the correct descriptive word in the sense that the Columbia River gathers water from every point of the compass before slipping through narrow Wallula Gap on the area's south boundary. But a basin it does not look to be. Only the Cascade Mountains to the west are close or high enough to look like a wall, and it is they that squeeze rain out of the clouds so that much of the land between rivers is parched and dry. What is more, the basin's floor is full of slow-wearing, sharp-edged basalt, much of it in the form of sheer walls.

Rugged terrain and vast size make this a loose sprawl of a place to get around in. Yakima, Wenatchee, and Moses Lake are the urban focal points. Most of the recreational opportunities are near them, save for the largest of them all—the great dam. It is way off by itself.

Weather. Yakima gives a fair impression of the regional climate: it averages 112 clear days a year, with another 87 partly cloudy. Measurable precipitation comes on 70 days in a typical season. Most of the annual 8 inches of precipitation arrives between November and March, much of it in the form of snow. Summers are warm, with 33 days at 90° F. and above (to a record 108°). First frosty nights come in mid-October. The last spring frost bites around April 20. In winter, the maximum temperature registers below 32° F. on 23 days; the minimum temperature sinks from there to –25° F. on 153 nights.

Farther north, in the Okanogan, summers are a shade cooler, winters a good deal sharper.

Another point to note is that a steady wind blows down the east slope of the Cascades in summer. At some places, such as Ellensburg, it never stops. In Yakima, Wenatchee, and Lake Chelan, the wind is typically an afternoon visitor. Farther from the mountains, it dwindles in both intensity and regularity.

Highways. Interstate 90—the major east-west route—is freeway all the way from Ellensburg through Moses Lake and beyond. To the north of I-90, two-lane U.S. 2 runs in more intimate contact with local farmlands. State 20, still farther north, tends to run in orchard and rangeland on the west side of the basin, then in forested mountain terrain on the east.

U.S. 97 runs north and south, sticking close to the Cascade foothills no matter where rivers might wander. Except for a short bit of freeway near Wenatchee, it is all broad two-lane roads, most of it straight and reasonably level, down to Ellensburg. From there, I-82 continues as freeway. No other north-south route is so direct as U.S. 97, but state highways farther east tend to be well-paved and wide.

Grand Coulee and Lesser Coulees

Grand Coulee Dam again plugs a narrow gap of the Columbia River course that was filled by ice during a great ice age. The ice dam forced a flooding river out into new channels, which are now known as Grand Coulee, Moses Coulee, Cheney Coulee, and others.

Today the river, back in its original channel, and the old alternate channels form a radiating web of streams and lakes rich in recreational development, all of them with Grand Coulee Dam as a sort of hub. Franklin D. Roosevelt Lake runs upstream behind the dam and far to the east of it (see page 125). Banks Lake occupies much of Grand Coulee; a chain of smaller lakes fills most of what is left. All of these waters have fish; most have campsites and boat launches.

Washington

See additional maps on pages 108, 109, and 112.

Grand Coulee Dam

Anyone who ever ran 2½ yards of concrete through a half-bag mixer to build a driveway will be interested to know that Grand Coulee Dam contains 11,975,521 cubic yards of the stuff.

The structure is 5,233 feet long and stands 550 feet high from streambed to top.

The combined generating capacity of its three main powerplants is 6,180,000 kilowatts. A set of reversible pump-generators, normally used to push 1,948 cubic feet of water per second up to Banks Lake, can add 314,000 kilowatts to the total.

Most of the water pumped up to Banks does not come back down, though. Banks is at the head of a 500,000-acre irrigation system that extends down to the Oregon border.

Self-guided tours cross the dam's top and continue down inside it amid awesome thrummings of generators and pumps. After sundown during the summer, in a sound-and-light show of overwhelming magnitude, colored lights play across the spillways and the torrents of water plummeting down them. (A drought in the mid-1970s dried up the spectacle for a time, proving that the river is finite, to the surprise of many.) A visitor center faces the spillways. Inside it, relief maps and displays explain the scope of river drainage and the dam's role in it. The two largest motels in the area also face the spillways.

Banks Lake

Grand Coulee Dam is pretty much a manmade wonder. Banks Lake is a remarkable cooperation of ancient natural history and contemporary human work. With a little help from two small dams, the irrigation reservoir fills 25 miles of Upper Grand Coulee. This coulee was originally scoured by the river, then left dry when melting ice allowed the stream to resume its usual course.

For visitors, the irrigation function plays a dim second to fishing and boating. A great many fishermen regard the oft-stocked lake as the state's most reliable source of trout.

Steamboat Rock State Park. A long, curving peninsula cuts away from the eastern shore of Banks Lake close to its midpoint, ending in a massive rock. Steamboat Rock State Park occupies most of that peninsula. The 900-acre park has 100 hookups, a boat launch, and a sheltered moorage. From May through August or September, fishermen and boaters dominate. As bird hunting begins in the Pacific Flyway, late-season fishermen compete with hunters for space.

Hiking trails wander from the green lawns of the campsite area up onto the rock after which the park is named. Incidentally, hallucinating under a midday sun is about the only way to see a steamboat in the long basalt outcrop.

Other access points. Electric City, at the north end of the lake near Grand Coulee Dam, also has a boat launch and marina.

At the south end of the lake, where U.S. 2 crosses an earth dam, the town of Coulee City has a camper park, boat launch, and moorage.

Dry Falls Area

Just south of what is now Banks Lake, the ice-age Columbia River, running 3 miles wide, plunged 400 feet over a falls before boiling on southward through the deep channel now called Lower Grand Coulee. The ancient waterfall is now Dry Falls, a dramatic landmark. In the old channel below lies a skein of trout-stocked small lakes. Much of this is packaged neatly as Sun Lakes State Park, one of the most-visited single parks in the Washington State system.

Dry Falls. The falls ran out of water after the ice melted at the present site of Grand Coulee Dam, allowing the Columbia to regain its original, more westerly streambed. Now visitors at the lofty observation points along one rim can only try to visualize a waterfall 3½ miles wide and thrice as high as Niagara. A state park visitor center alongside State 17 explains in detail how this dramatic landscape was formed and re-formed by the changing river. A trail leads down one basalt wall to any of several small lakes, then south a mile to the main camping area of the state park.

Sun Lakes State Park. The active center of the park runs along the shore of Park Lake, one of a dozen pools in the ancient riverbed. Here, nestled close together, are rental cabins; almost 200 campsites (18 hookups); a riding stable; the nine-hole, play-early (no shade) golf course; a swimming beach; and rental boats.

The park covers over 4,000 acres. Between Park Lake and Dry Falls, hiking and equestrian trails thread among four small lakes. Below Park Lake are the larger Blue, Alkali, and Lenore lakes.

Lake Lenore Caves State Park. The little strip of land separating Lenore and Alkali lakes carries a short road leading east from State 17 to Lake Lenore Caves. The caves, shallow cuts into a basalt bluff, apparently served as a rudimentary motel for Indians traveling through the area 11,000 to 4,000 years ago.

Summer Falls State Park. From May through October, irrigation water from Banks Lake is pumped over Summer Falls on its way to work. Tables and a lawn at the base of the falls make the park a memorable picnic site when the falls are running. The park, east of Lenore Lake, is on a local road that parallels State 17. From the north, Summer Falls can be reached directly from Coulee City. From Soap Lake on the south, head east on State 28 about 8 miles to the posted turn.

Soap Lake

Soap Lake had its heyday in the 1930s and 1940s, when mineral waters and mud baths were in greater vogue than now. Rather than change to suit more hectic times, the little resort community continues at its relaxed pace, waiting for the rest of the world to slow down.

The lake waters are extremely buoyant as well as mineralized, which makes them as popular with vacationing families in search of sun and safe swimming for kids as with seekers of spas.

Moses Lake and Ephrata

Moses Lake—town and body of water—sits at the bottom of the coulee country, 80 miles south of Grand Coulee Dam and 35 miles south of Sun Lakes State Park, but smack on freeway I-90.

The community grew from a sleepy hamlet to a sprawling small city when a U.S. Air Force Base (since decommissioned) was established there.

Agriculture has replaced airmen as the backbone of the local economy. Amid fine lakes for boating, fishing, and bird hunting, Moses Lake also serves as headquarters for outdoor recrea-

tion. And its freeway location has made it a useful overnight stopping point for east-west travelers.

Accommodations. Motels congregate on Business Loop I-90, especially at the west edge of town near Exit 176. Restaurants are near the motels.

Attractions. Adam East Museum, located downtown at 5th and Balsam, houses paleontology exhibits from the coulee country and a large collection of Indian materials from the region. Admission is free. A picnic park adjoins the museum.

Local settlement by European descendants is recorded in the Grant County Historical Museum at Ephrata, a farm community 17 miles west and north of Moses Lake. The museum is open May through September; admission is free.

The old air base north of town, now Grant County Airport, is a principal training field for wide-body aircraft pilots. Every day, Boeing 747s practice touch-and-goes by the scores, accompanied by smaller numbers of DC-10s and other planes. For insatiable jumbo jet watchers, the field has an observation deck and a restaurant. The airport is accessible via State 17 to Ephrata.

At Ephrata, for contrast, a small field has become home to a considerable number of glider pilots.

Parks and recreation. McCosh Park, 3 blocks south of Business I-90, has a fine municipal swimming pool, playground equipment, night-lighted tennis courts, picnic tables, and lawns.

Moses Lake State Park faces town across the main body of the lake. On the west shore right next to the freeway, the day-use park has tree-shaded picnic sites, a swimming beach, and a summer food concession.

Shallow, sun-warm Moses Lake supports a mixed population of water-skiers, swimmers, hydroplaners, and fishermen (the latter mostly after bass, perch, and crappie, and occasionally trout). Equipment for all these pursuits can be rented at several lakeshore motels, commercial camper parks, or marinas.

Potholes State Park is the camper's nearest resource in a public park. Twenty miles south from I-90 Exit 179, the park has 126 campsites (60 hookups), a boat launch, and a marina. The shallow man-made lake is at its best for fishing and other recreation in spring.

The unique Grand Coulee

Many years after its debut, the key link in a vast power chain and 2-million-acre irrigation project is still growing in size.

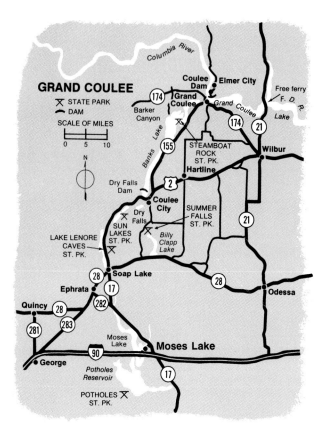

GRAND COULEE

✕ STATE PARK
⌒ DAM
SCALE OF MILES
0   5   10

In Ephrata, 17 miles north and west of Moses Lake, Oasis Park has usefully central campsites for all of the recreational and fishing waters from Potholes on the south to Banks Lake on the north.

Dozens of small lakes and streams offer excellent fishing in this region, and also to the north toward Banks Lake. Local sporting goods stores are invaluable sources of information about specialized requirements and seasons. Grant County maintains public access on 30 lakes and several connecting streams.

By the Riverside

As vast as it is, the Columbia River below Grand Coulee Dam becomes relatively elusive for recreationists all the way down to the Tri-Cities area. Only rarely do visitors have opportunities to get into or onto the river.

In spite of that, a mixture of towns, hydroelectric dams, and parks provides a surprisingly diverse set of ways to think about the river and to use it. In addition, the resort end of Lake Chelan—a kind of tributary to the Columbia—is a more

than adequate replacement for watery recreation in the main river. Wenatchee serves most usefully as an urban focal point for all the rest.

Lake Chelan

Fjordlike, Lake Chelan snakes its way deep into the Cascade Mountains. The mountainous end is remote, nearly wilderness, but the end nearest the Columbia River supports a lively resort community devoted mostly to boating, both power and sail.

Several major motels line the north shore along the stub road, State 150. Several more motels fit between U.S. 97 and the south shore.

The town of Chelan maintains a large camping park at the edge of town on State 150. The park has picnic tables, a swimming beach, play lawns, and a pair of lighted tennis courts.

On a bluff high above, Lake Chelan Golf & Country Club (18 holes; 6,300 yards; par 72) bumps and rolls across a narrow bench, a fair test even when the scenery does not cause lapses of concentration.

Lake Chelan State Park, 9 miles west of Chelan via U.S. 97 and a spur road, tucks almost 150 campsites (17 hookups) into 127 wooded lakeshore acres. The park includes a boat launch and swimming beach, as well as a day-use picnic area.

Chelan's most famous attraction, though, is a day-long excursion trip by boat to Stehekin at the head of the lake. Many make the round trip just to savor scenery of a high order. Many more debark at Stehekin or one of the intermediate points to hike through that scenery. (See page 93 for further details on the upper lake.)

Although marinas at Chelan rent small boats, they recommend against up-lake trips. The long, narrow cut into the mountains gathers enough wind to produce very rough water in the upper reaches.

Wenatchee

Years ago, the local newspaper began referring to Wenatchee as the apple capital of the world and the buckle of the Pacific Northwest power belt. It is no poetic phrase, but, then, it takes no poetic license. It speaks the plain truth on both counts.

On the Columbia, the city is flanked by an impressive collection of hydroelectric dams both upstream and down. Down to tiny scraps, the region's arable lands bear orchards. Indeed, the intensity of local cultivation rivals that in mountainous Switzerland; some narrow benches in steep basalt cliffs hold only a few trees each.

Wenatchee has one other major function. At the crossroads of U.S. highways 97 and 2, it serves as gateway into the Cascades, the coulee country, and the Okanogan, and also as a stopover point for travelers on longer journeys to or from the coast, or north into British Columbia.

Accommodations. The main street north of the main shopping district holds an amazing number of motels, several of them large. East Wenatchee adds one large motel and several small ones to the roster.

Attractions. Wenatchee's two great attractions are a lush garden wrested out of one of the less hospitable basalt crags in the region, and a dam with a fine museum buried deep inside its concrete mass.

Ohme Gardens, a family enterprise since 1929, covers 9 acres of a lofty bluff with evergreens, heather, mosses, and several species of shrubs and alpine flowers. All these elements blend to approximate a high alpine meadow down in the hot, dry basin. Irrigation in the form of streams and pools is the key.

A spur road west off U.S. 97, 4 miles north of town, leads up to the parking lot. There is an admission fee.

Rocky Reach Dam, owned by the local utility district, is but a hop and skip up U.S. 97 from Ohme Gardens. A picnic ground and an eye-level look into the fish ladder are standard visitor fare. The welcome surprise is a three-part museum within the dam's main structure. One part is an agreeable look into local geology, and a second area offers some revealing displays of past Indian cultures. But the greatest space is given over to the Gallery of Electricity, where inventive displays explain the whole history of electricity from Ben Franklin's kite to some of the wizard microcircuitry of the space age. Along the way, to the great delight of kids, all kinds of obsolete electrical contrivances can be made to cheep, or growl, or give light.

Parks and recreation. One city and one county park provide excellent resources for picnics, playgrounds, and tennis. Pioneer Park, southwest of the downtown at Fuller and Russell, nestles under a dense, cooling grove of mature trees. Its picnic tables and barbecues are lighted for evening use, as are two tennis courts. (Two blocks away, Wenatchee High has eight more courts, unlighted.) Across the river in East Wenatchee, Eastmont County Park, at Grant Road and Georgia, is younger and more open. It has an imaginative playground, ample picnic tables, four lighted tennis courts, and an indoor swimming pool.

Seven miles north of East Wenatchee on U.S. 2, Lincoln Rock State Park overlooks Lake Entiat and Turtle Rock Island (accessible by boat). A rock across Lake Entiat is thought to resemble the profile of Abraham Lincoln. The park, which has

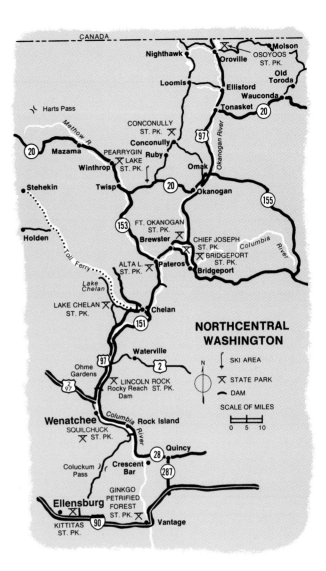

27 campsites, is popular for water-related activities. Rocky Reach Dam is just one mile south of the park.

Five miles south of town on the west side of the river, Three Lakes Golf Course (18 holes; 5,269 yards; par 69) tucks into a serene little valley all its own. Nine miles south on the east side of the river, Rock Island Golf Course (9 holes, 18 tees; 5,841 yards; par 71) plays flatter, but with water close by. Other courses within reach are at Chelan and Crescent Bar (see page 111).

Cashmere

Cashmere perches just at the edge of the steep Cascade foothills, 13 miles west of Wenatchee on U.S. Highway 2.

The main street of Cashmere is a picture-book re-creation of an old-fashioned Middle America Main Street.

Cowboys and Indians

In Central Washington, the range-riding cowboy still exists. In every part of the state are Indians, many of whom work as cowboys. Rodeos (below) are easy to find. Some Indian encampments (right) allow visitors (see page 68).

The principal local industry is fruit growing and processing. The most famous form taken by local fruit is Aplets and Cotlets, candies made by Liberty Orchards in their factory one block south of the main street, across from the train depot. Visitors to the factory can take a 15-minute tour.

Cashmere's other specific attraction is the Chelan County Historical Museum, east of town on U.S. 2. Upstairs is a gathering of pioneer and Indian artifacts. Downstairs is a series of re-created interiors. Behind the main building is an entire village of typical frontier structures.

Crescent Bar

At the foot of a 700-foot palisade a few miles west of Quincy on State 28, the road to Wenatchee, Crescent Bar is a commercial camper resort with great appeal to power boaters, water-skiers, and all who enjoy vacationing in recreational vehicles.

An oasis of lawns, trees, and beaches, it has 200 hookups. Many are leased the year around, but overnighters can find space.

The development also has a 9-hole, 2,873-yard, par 35 golf course.

Vantage

Two state parks and Wanapum Dam make this once-dreary landscape one of the genuine oases along I-90's long, mostly dry run across eastern Washington.

Ginkgo Petrified Forest State Park, just north of the freeway on the Columbia's west bank, explores local geology, especially volcanic history and related petrified forests. A visitor center contains petrified wood from dozens of species the world around to compare with the local prehistoric forest of ginkgos. Outside the center, a grove of living ginkgos shades a pleasant picnic area.

The main body of the park and the petrified trees lie some hundreds of yards north of the visitor center. It is a preserve—no petrified wood or other material can be taken from it. But the opportunities to see a petrified forest are excellent.

Wanapum State Park sits south of the freeway, still on the west bank. This 451-acre park has 50 campsites (all with R.V. hookups), a spacious riverside picnic lawn, and a swimming beach and boat launch.

Wanapum Dam is visible just downstream from the park, but access to it is on an east-shore road, State 243. It has the usual powerhouse and fish ladder tours, but, like Rocky Reach near Wenatchee, it is most notable for a fine museum. This one deals with humanity's long use of the Columbia River, beginning with Indians and running through the steamboat era into the present.

The Okanogan

Several river valleys in Central Washington are genuine cowboy country. Dry, rolling hills make good rangeland but not much else. The Okanogan River valley is the classic example. It also is the access route to fishing and hunting country.

This place should not be confused with the Okanagan, the northward extension of the valley into British Columbia. Much more changes at the border than the spelling of the name. On the B.C. side, three large lakes have been developed into dense resort areas, sunny escapes for Vancouverites. On Washington's side of the border, however, agriculture and cattle ranching remain the foremost activities, almost the only ones. Visitors come here in search of rugged wilderness, or dude ranching with far more emphasis on ranching than dude.

U.S. 97 burrows, straight and quick, from Brewster—where the Okanogan flows into the Columbia—north through Okanogan, Omak, and Oroville to the border. On either side of the route, camping parks make poking into the back country easy for fishermen, hunters, or seekers of ghost towns. Motels in the three towns are neither numerous nor large. Reservations are wise, especially at rodeo time (mid-August).

Parks in the Okanogan

A cluster of parks flanks the mouth of the Okanogan River where it joins the Columbia River.

Fort Okanogan State Park Museum sketches a quick history of the region through dioramas, photos, and small tools. It begins with Indian life before whites came and roams through time to the present, giving special attention to fur traders and riverboaters. Outside, sheltered picnic tables look down from a bluff to the riverbanks.

A few miles up the Columbia River from this site, Bridgeport State Park nestles into a shallow defile. Irrigation water from the nearby Chief Joseph Dam allows the park to maintain spreading lawns and shading trees all around its 28 campsites. The softness is a visual dessert in this hard, dry country.

Just outside the park gates, Lake Woods Golf Course (9 holes; 2,574 yards; par 34) extends the green carpet over another few acres.

An equal distance downstream from Fort Okanogan, Alta Lake State Park tucks into a narrow valley 2 miles up the Methow River from U.S. 97 at Pateros. The nearly 200 campsites (16 hookups) in this park shelter under tall pines alongside the lake. There is a swimming beach.

Alta Lake Golf Course (9 holes; 3,400 yards; par 36) adjoins the park.

In the Okanogan Valley proper, the city of Omak operates 73-acre East Side Park next to its rodeo grounds. The park has campsites, cooking shelters and picnic tables, a swimming pool, playground equipment, tennis courts, baseball and soccer fields, and even a bike track.

Conconully State Park, several miles into the hills west of Omak, has about 80 campsites (10 hookups) in 81 acres. Conconully Lake attracts swimmers and fishermen.

Almost at the Canadian border, Osoyoos Lake State Park, a mile north of Oroville on U.S. 97, comes closest to the resort character of British Columbia's share of the valley. In 41 acres it has 86 campsites, a spreading picnic ground, and boat launches (for water-skiers as much as fishermen), plus nearby stores and restaurants.

In addition to these major parks, the Okanogan hill country is dotted with state forest and national forest campgrounds (also see page 94).

Gold Country Ghost Towns

The Okanogan had a brief heyday as the site of a gold rush late in the 19th century. Scattered along tributary streams in the valley are a handful of ghost towns from that era.

Conconully once was the county seat; now it is only a scattering of rock walls from old courthouse vaults. It adjoins Conconully State Park.

Loomis is several miles north of Conconully via a rough road. It can be reached more easily from U.S. 97 at Ellisford.

A gravel road leads west from Oroville to Nighthawk. Actually, the road leads to the Similkameen River. A footbridge crosses the stream, giving access to abandoned buildings of the Ruby Mine and a leaky-seamed log cabin.

Molson is 13 miles east of Oroville. Developed more than most, with more surviving buildings, it most closely conforms to the movie image of a ghost town. It also has the richest collection of junk for kids to pick through.

The Space Age in Okanogan

Because the region was settled late and only sparsely, it has fewer radios than most of the U.S. For this reason a COMSAT earth station is located on a bluff north of Brewster.

A visitor center at the station explains in a lucid, friendly way how satellite communication works.

Brewster Flat Road leads to the station from the town of Brewster. Another road cuts west from U.S. 97 to it. The visitor center is open daily.

The Yakima Valley

The Yakima Valley is one of those improbably rich agricultural basins that crop up here and there in the world's temperate zones. This one is full of orchards, vineyards, hop fields, and more.

Along I-82 between Yakima and the Tri-Cities, and elsewhere in the Yakima Valley, are numerous wineries. Wine tour information is available at the Yakima Valley Visitor & Convention Bureau.

The City of Yakima

Yakima, commercial center of the valley, means to bustle. It does. Most of its visitors come to do agricultural business. No few come for conven-

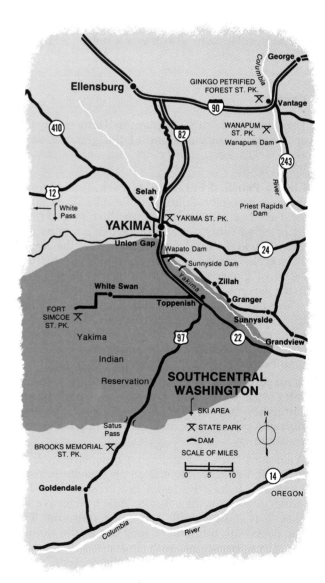

tions. Seattleites frequently use Yakima as a handy escape to sun.

Accommodations. Most of Yakima's plentiful motels run along North First, the connector between freeway U.S. 12 and downtown. The convention center is downtown on Yakima Avenue, which crosses First to form the city's principal intersection. Restaurants are plentiful along both streets.

Attractions. The Yakima Valley Museum, at 21st and Tieton Drive in the southwest quarter of town, has uncommonly well-staged historical exhibits concerning both Yakima Indians and white settlers, but its crowning display is the Gannon wagon collection. The diverse genius of horse-drawn vehicle designers has few better forums than this. A lumbering Conestoga stands a few feet and several light years away from a nimble trap, but not such a great distance from a charabanc. There is, of course, a surrey with fringe on top.

The museum, adjacent to an agreeable picnic park, is open Wednesday through Sunday.

Outside museum walls, the Yakima Interurban Trolley Lines runs a pair of authentic antique trolley cars along more than 19 miles of operating track. They run through the countryside, past fruit orchards and historical sights.

Parks and recreation. Yakima's excellent park system includes a Japanese garden and plentiful tennis courts and horseshoe pits among its many facilities. A high point is the Yakima River Greenway, 3,600 acres along the Yakima River east of town, which includes bicycle and foot trails, beaches, picnic spots, and playfields.

Public play golf courses are not abundant in a region where farmlands cannot be too large or too well watered, but there are two. Sun-Tides Golf Course (18 holes; 6,215 yards; par 70) is a level, young layout 4 miles northwest of downtown on U.S. 12. Westwood West Golf Course (9 holes; 2,626 yards; par 35) is older and rolls a bit. It is 5 miles west of town on Tieton Drive.

For those who prefer spectator sports, Yakima Meadows presents thoroughbred and quarter-horse racing along a one-mile course.

Yakima Sportsman State Park occupies 230 acres near the river a mile east of Yakima, just off Interstate 82, the freeway from Ellensburg. It has 28 campsites (36 hookups), and a sizable picnic ground with kitchens and sheltered tables. The park also has a playground and fishing ponds for children under 15.

The Lower Valley

Downstream from the city of Yakima, the dry hills spread farther apart and the irrigated valley floor grows green.

The Cowboy at His Best

Partly the rodeo is a joyous tribute to occupational skills. Partly it is a backward glance at the romance of the old west. But mostly it is a rip-roaring show that pits puny man against mighty beast.

Washington has plenty of working cowboys roaming its rangeland, most of it forming a long arc from the southeast corner up through the Columbia basin and farther north through the Okanogan country.

There are junior rodeos, an intercollegiate circuit, and—at the top of the prize-money heap—Rodeo Cowboys Association epics.

It is wise to write ahead to the local chamber of commerce for rodeo dates or to Washington's Tourist Development Division for its annual calendar.

MAY

Washington State U. NIRA Rodeo, Pullman, 1st weekend.
49er Parade and Rodeo, Winthrop, 1st weekend.
Colorama Rodeo, Grand Coulee, 2nd weekend.
Tonasket Rodeo, Tonasket, 3rd weekend.
Winthrop Rodeo, Winthrop, last weekend.

JUNE

Roy Pioneer Rodeo, Roy, 1st weekend.
All Indian Rodeo, White Swan, 2nd week.
Little Britches Rodeo, Silverdale, 3rd weekend.
Colville Rodeo, Colville, 3rd weekend.

JULY

Loggerodeo, Sedro Woolley, 1st week.
Junior Rodeo, Everson, 2nd weekend.
Cheney Rodeo, Spokane, 2nd weekend.
Lake Chelan Rodeo, Chelan, 3rd weekend.
North Whidbey Stampede, Oak Harbor, last weekend.

AUGUST

PQHA Junior Rodeo, Colville, 1st weekend.
Omak Stampede and Suicide Race, Omak, 2nd weekend.
Saddle Club Rodeo, Long Beach, 2nd weekend.
Sun Downs RCA Rodeo, Kennewick, last wknd.

SEPTEMBER

Ellensburg Rodeo, Ellensburg, 1st weekend.
Rodeo, Winthrop, 1st weekend.
Roy Pioneer Rodeo, Roy, 1st weekend.

This is the heart of Washington's sprightly young table wine industry, and home of a hop industry with an international market among brewers who care. These specialized crops share space with a variety of tree fruit, melons, tomatoes, potatoes, sugar beets, and asparagus.

In harvest time, visitors can buy a bonanza at roadside.

Washington State University's Irrigated Agriculture Research and Extension Center at Prosser, 54 miles southeast of Yakima, offers an unparalleled opportunity for gardeners to find out all they wish to know about growing all the above, and roses and chrysanthemums as well. The center is open to visitors on weekdays. Signs show the way from downtown Prosser.

Prosser City Park, right downtown, is a useful picnic stop. The Benton County Historical Museum adjoins it. It is open daily, except Monday.

The largest concentration of Yakima Valley wineries is in Prosser. Tours and tastings are offered on a regular basis by Yakima River (509) 786-2805, and Hogue (509) 786-4557. Call for appointments at Chinook (509) 786-2725, Hinzerling (509) 786-2163, and Pontin Del Rey (509) 786-4449.

Useful Addresses in Central Washington

- Coulee Dam National Recreation Area Coulee Dam, WA 99116
- U.S. Bureau of Reclamation, P.O. Box 815, Code 140, Ephrata, WA 98823

Chambers of Commerce

- P.O. Box 343, Cashmere, WA 98815
- P.O. Box 66, Coulee Dam, WA 99115
- P.O. Box 760, Grand Coulee, WA 99133
- Lake Chelan, P.O. Box 216 Chelan, WA 98816
- 436 N. Sprague, Ellensburg, WA 98926
- P.O. Box 1093, Moses Lake, WA 98837
- P.O. Box 1125, Okanogan, WA 98840
- P.O. Box 536, Oroville, WA 98844
- 33 E. Larch, Othello, WA 99344
- P.O. Box 433, Soap Lake, WA 98851
- Wenatchee Visitor Bureau, P.O. Box 850, Wenatchee, WA 98801
- Yakima Valley Visitor Bureau, P.O. Box 124, Yakima, WA 98907

Visitable wineries dot the landscape all the way from Yakima to the Tri-Cities.

The architecturally dramatic Yakima Nation Cultural Center flanks U.S. 97 just at the western outskirts of Toppenish. Here the story of the Yakima Indians is told. A library and theater supplement the museum, which is open daily all year. Telephone (509) 865-2800.

About 5 miles south of town on U.S. 97, the Toppenish National Wildlife Refuge is home to many species of birds. A nature trail and tours are available; call the interpretive center at (509) 865-2405 for more information.

From Toppenish, a spur road leads 30 miles across the Yakima reservation to 200-acre Fort Simcoe State Historic Park. Several mid-1800s buildings have been restored and furnished; picnicking facilities are available. The park is open daily May through October.

Yakima Canyon

The Yakima River rises high in the Cascades but does not carve its own valley until it gets to Yakima, the city. Between Ellensburg and Yakima, it reaches its scenic high point in the Yakima River Canyon.

The canyon used to be the main route between the two cities. Now a freeway up on the ridge top has freed the old canyon road from commercial duty, allowing pokeabouts to drive it for pleasure.

The river is quick but not rough. Each summer literally thousands of Washingtonians float down it on rafts, inner tubes, and other flexible craft.

The state has proposed the canyon as a park.

Ellensburg

This town is noted for three things in particular: it is home to the granddaddy of all Washington rodeos, on Labor Day weekend (see page 113); it is home to Central Washington University; and it is the geographic center of the state. (The precise spot, at Eighth and D, is marked.) In addition, each May the National Western Art Show and Auction comes to town.

In this quiet, attractive town, historical preservation and renovation have been the policy. The Ellensburg Historic District includes about 20 Victorian buildings. Descriptive maps are available at the Kittitas County Historical Museum, at East Third and Pine streets.

Just outside town, the Olmstead Place is a Washington State Parks heritage site. It is a well-preserved example of a 19th-century farmstead including the original log cabin and some simple farm buildings. The farm is 4 miles east of Ellensburg via the Kittitas Highway, which parallels I-90 along its north side.

Basking in the sun

The southern tip of Lake Chelan is a thoroughly developed resort with fine beaches, boating, golf, and more. The city of Chelan's park (below) is one of four in the area. Otherwise, the district is one focal point of Central Washington's large, flourishing apple industry, famous for both Golden (left) and Red Delicious.

Washington's eastern boundary—
too little explored—holds
surprises in rich variety

The Eastern

This rugged part of the state has some extraordinary natural and man-made scenery. It's famous for its rolling wheat fields, while its dense pine forests and hundreds of lakes are less well known to visitors.

The Kettle Mountains, for example, may not be as famous as the Cascades, but the highest pass in Washington, at 5,575 feet, is in the Kettles near Republic. The Snake River may not be as voluminous as the Columbia, but it runs a dramatic 2,000 feet below the rim of its canyon not far west of Clarkston.

Fishermen, backpackers, and others who enjoy the outdoors will find fish-filled lakes, wooded campsites, and unspoiled countryside.

Also in the region, as throughout the state, is lively evidence of the conflict and cooperation between Indian and European-derived cultures.

The major highway through the region, Interstate 90, invites drivers to stay on it with its guaranteed speed. But collectors of back roads must go a long way to find better or more diverse ones than those here, which ramble through forests, along great rivers, near small gold mines, and past huge farms.

I-90 leads straight into Spokane, the hub of the Inland Empire—an agricultural, mining, and trading realm that takes in much of eastern Washington and parts of Oregon, Idaho, Montana, and even Canada. The college towns of Walla Walla and Pullman offer urban respite in the wide landscape, as do several agricultural and mining communities.

Weather. Spokane has a genuine four-season climate. Summers are hot and dry. Winters are cold and fairly wet. Spring and fall lead up to the following seasons in traditional form. The rest of the region follows Spokane's pattern closely, except where high elevation tempers summer and exaggerates winter.

In summer, the city can expect 20 days at 90°F. or more (to an all-time record of 108°). Very little of the annual average 18 inches of precipitation falls between May and October.

Cold is more pervasive. Spokane experiences an average of 138 freezing nights a year, six of them reaching 0°F. or below. The record low is −20°. Snow is not uncommon but seldom gets deep.

In higher terrain to the north, summer is cooler and winter more bitter. South of Spokane, summers are as warm or warmer, but winters do not have quite so much bite.

Highways. Interstate 90 is the great flattened, straightened east-west corridor. Its exits are numbered to correspond to mileposts, which start at 1 in Seattle, reach 283 at Spokane, and finish at 296 just before the Idaho border.

U.S. 2, roughly parallel to and not far north of I-90, runs mostly in pleasant farm country from Grand Coulee to Spokane. Still farther north, State 20 is tough to drive but offers a rewarding east-west route through farm, timber, and mining country, all scenic.

U.S. 395 from Spokane to the Canadian border is the great north-south axis.

Going south from Spokane, U.S. 195 is the major route all the way to Clarkston. U.S. 12 runs east-west in the southeast quarter from Clarkston through Walla Walla to the Tri-Cities.

All these routes except I-90 are two-laners. The federal routes are consistently wide, with wide shoulders. State roads may be narrower.

Spokane

Spokane, Washington's second-largest city, has never gone for flash at the expense of livability. Prosperous agricultural, lumber, and mining interests built a sober downtown between 1880 and 1940, using more red brick than anything else. In recent years, steel and concrete have been added, but the downtown continues to have a comfortable texture and scale.

The world exposition of 1974 sparked some new excitement (and renewed livability). The expo site, Riverfront Park, is in the tradition of Spokane's fine park system. In the center of the city, it serves

See additional maps on pages 121 and 124.

Seattle Spokane

as a replacement for industrial decay and urban blight. The expo's opera house provides a long-term home for the performing arts.

Along with the downtown face-lift and new facilities have come growth in the range and liveliness of the city's cultural life. Like Seattle, Spokane seems to have benefitted in many long-term ways from its world's fair.

The physical drama in downtown Spokane comes from the Spokane River, which slips quietly into town from the east, but leaves the main shopping area as a thunderous series of falls. Some of the city's unifying bridges cross within awesomely close range.

For visitors, the city offers some fine preservations of its early wealth, a wide-ranging museum of Indian history, a tribute to native son Bing Crosby, concrete souvenirs of its spirited fair,

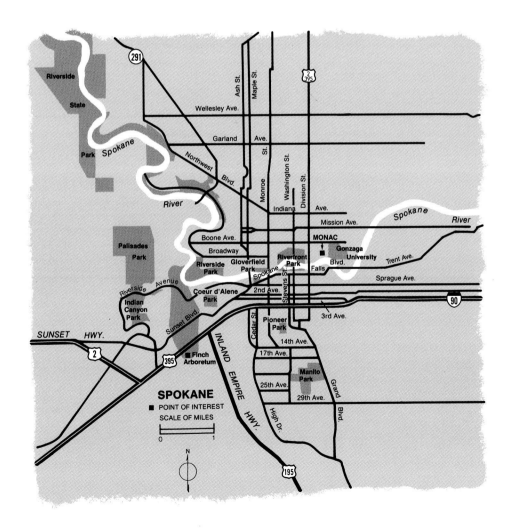

Spokane's special parks

In Spokane, formal garden in Manito Park (right) offers serenity, while circling carousel (below) in downtown park makes for glee.

and—typical of all Washington cities—abundant outdoor recreation in and near town.

Spokane, astride Interstate 90, also serves as a gateway to all the great outdoors of eastern Washington as well as Idaho's lake-filled panhandle.

Accommodations. Downtown boasts a sizable collection of hotels and motels near the Spokane River, which sluices through the heart of the city. Most of these are on or near Division Street, accessible from the freeway at Exit 281. Another cluster of motels lies eastward along Sprague Avenue (parallel to the freeway and just north of it), handy to the Interstate Fairgrounds. A third grouping of motels flanks I-90 to the west, mostly along Sunset Boulevard.

Attractions. Spokane can be thought of as a series of parks, with Riverfront Park as the hub of the radiating set of older, mostly Olmstead-designed greenbelt. "Downtown" in the sense of clusters of buildings has its center right by Riverfront Park.

A good way to get an overview of the city is to take the driving tour that begins at the corner of Stevens Street and Sprague Avenue. Signs lead the way to many of the city's attractions.

Downtown Riverfront Park, site of Expo '74, offers greenbelt dotted with urban attractions. Side by side, with a covered walkway linking them, are the Convention Center and the Opera House, home of the Spokane Symphony and the ballet (for information on their performances and other arts activities, call (509) 747-ARTS). The Eastern Washington Science Center features hands-on regional exhibits. A rink attracts roller skaters in the summer, ice skaters in winter. Pavilion rides are a delight for children. At the Imax Theater, a 5-story screen conveys dazzling special effects. The Loof Carousel's hand-carved steeds spin within a glass-walled shelter. May through October, a public market and arts and crafts marketplace operate on park grounds.

But the best part of Riverfront Park is the clear-flowing river itself. Paths meander toward, beside, and over it. One footbridge gives pulse-raising looks at the thunderous rapids of Spokane Falls; another takes walkers by placid pools complete with waterfowl. Look carefully and you'll see sculpture rising like islands from the water. For another perspective entirely, a gondola ride swings up and over the tumbling rapids.

Rain, sleet, snow, and hail need not deter Spokane shoppers. On the downtown side of Riverfront Park are entrances to a 15-block system of second-story walkways, called the Skywalk, connecting department stores, specialty shops, restaurants, and offices. On the opposite side of Riverfront Park, just south of the coliseum, a former flour mill houses shops and restaurants.

West of downtown in historic Browne's Addi-tion, Cheney Cowles Memorial Museum at West 2316 First Avenue holds exhibits of local natural history and Indian and pioneer history. It also has fine arts galleries emphasizing regional artists. Next door, the Tudor-style Campbell House preserves a wealthy mode of living from the late 19th century. Mining magnate A. B. Campbell had his 20-room showplace built in 1898. Both buildings are owned and operated by the Eastern Washington Historical Society; they are open daily except Monday.

Browne's Addition is a neighborhood of fine old houses, many of which are being restored. It is worth a walking tour.

On the other side of the Spokane River, the Museum of Native American Cultures (MONAC) looks into the lives and culture of Indians of the Americas. The displays are best appreciated by starting at the top floor. Located at East 200 Cataldo between the Division Street bridge and Gonzaga University, the center is open Tuesday through Saturday. There is a nominal charge.

On the Gonzaga campus is a small museum holding memorabilia from the singing career of native son Bing Crosby. It is open weekdays 8 A.M. to 5 P.M. Start at the information office just inside the Administration Building main door.

Over on the south side of the freeway, at 12th Avenue and Grand, the soaring Gothic spires of St. John the Evangelist provide a look at an entirely different relationship of man to nature. Built in 1927, the building is one of few truly Gothic-style structures in the United States. Its walls lean toward each other, held apart only by lofty arches; its spires are medieval symbols of humanity's highest reach. The Episcopal cathedral is open to all visitors weekdays from 10 A.M. to 4 P.M.

On the hills above the cathedral is a neighborhood of fine homes. In the same general area is a fine view of the city from Cliff Park, off 13th Avenue.

Three Spokane wineries offer tours of their facilities and samples of their products. Call Latah Creek, (509) 926-0164, and Worden's, (509) 455-7835, for directions. Arbor Crest has tasting rooms in town and at the Cliff House, a 1924 home high on a nearby bluff. Call (509) 484-9463 to arrange a visit.

In-town parks and recreation. Riverfront Park is not alone in offering green space within the city. Manito Park, a cool, green oasis of gardens and playgrounds unequaled in Eastern Washington, rambles across a high ridge south of the freeway in this hilly city.

For gardeners the variety seems endless: formal Duncan Gardens, especially alive in May with the perfume of lilacs; Rose Hill, at its peak of bloom in June; a Japanese garden that surpasses seasons; and a greenhouse-conservatory sheltered from those seasons.

Out-of-towners can most readily get to the heart of these gardens, and also to picnic and play areas, by following Stevens Street south from downtown. Stevens bends to become Grand, which straightens out just before reaching the 18th Avenue entrance to the park.

The 65-acre John A. Finch Arboretum holds 2,000 labeled trees and shrubs representing more than 120 genera, 600 species and varieties. Major groups include 75 varieties of crabapple and 65 of lilacs. (Spokane has an ongoing love affair with lilacs, for which it is an almost flawless environment.) Plantings date from 1949.

The arboretum tucks itself between I-90 and the Sunset Highway west of downtown, between freeway exits 277 and 279. It is open daily.

Two of Spokane's fine municipal golf courses are almost as much gardens as the city's other parks. Indian Canyon Golf Course (18 holes; 6,256 yards; par 72) rolls along a heavily treed wall of the Latah Creek–Spokane River Watercourse just a few blocks from Finch Arboretum. Downriver Golf Course (18 holes; 5,833 yards; par 71) looks directly into the Spokane River from its lofty bluff at the exact northwest corner of the city, right next to Riverside State Park.

A third municipal course on the east side of town is newer, flatter Esmerelda (18 holes; 6,077 yards; par 70). Other public courses in the region include Hangman Valley (18 holes; 6,500 yards; par 71), 5 miles south of the city on U.S. 195; Sun Dance Golf course (18 holes; 6,000 yards; par 70), 3 miles north of Spokane on State 291; and Wandemere Golf Course (18 holes; 5,815 yards; par 69), 5 miles north of the city limits on U.S. 395.

In winter, cross-country skiing is available at city and county parks, as well as at golf courses. Call the park department for details.

The major spectator sports organizations are the Spokane Indians baseball team (a farm club for the San Diego Padres), Spokane Chiefs hockey, Playfair horse racing, Spokane Raceway auto racing, and Spokane Polo Club.

Suburban parks and recreation. Two huge state parks offer year-round recreation within easy reach of downtown Spokane. A zoo rounds out close-at-hand recreational opportunities.

Riverside State Park covers both banks of the Spokane River for several miles, beginning at the northwestern city limits and extending north beyond Nine Mile Falls. The nearly 6,000-acre park has over 100 campsites and abundant picnic sites in open groves of pine. Fishermen, in particular, favor the camping area.

At the north end of the park, Spokane House Interpretive Center includes a model of the 1810 North West Company trading post, established as the first permanent white settlement in Washington by explorer-geographer David Thompson.

Trails all through the park draw heavy use from hikers in the dry season, snowmobilers in winter.

Mt. Spokane State Park, 30 miles north and east of town, snugs right up to the Idaho state line. It is a major park summer and winter. Summers, the cool air on higher slopes draws picnickers and hikers. In winter, five double chair lifts and five rope tows serve groomed ski slopes with a total of 2,100 feet of vertical drop. Runs are lighted for night skiing. Cross-country skiers use summer's hiking trails. Condominium accommodations are available. State 206 leads north to the park; from I-90 Exit 289 the route is marked clearly.

The same Exit 289 leads to Spokane's Walk-In Wild Zoo, where a diverse collection of native animals and animals from similar environments lives without cages. Visitors stroll among them, able to touch the quieter species but kept at safe distances from the others by moats, gullies, and other natural-seeming barriers.

Southeast Corner

Washington's sparsely settled southeast corner offers a mixture of untamable wilderness, highly groomed farmland, and well-polished civility.

Far the greatest proportion of the space rests untamed. Hunters and fishermen flock to the region for big game, birds, and trout living in this wild region. Great, rolling expanses of farmland take up most of the rest. Civility cloaks the towns of Walla Walla and Pullman and their college campuses. Walla Walla in particular has a long history as an outpost of European civilization in a rugged land.

Two roads serve all three worlds.

Starting from the Columbia River near the Oregon border, U.S. 12 passes through the wheat, asparagus, and sweet onion fields on either side of the college town of Walla Walla. Then it curves tightly through hilly, oft-times wild country en route to Clarkston at the Idaho line. Just south of Clarkston—with its Hells Canyon excursions, active art colony, and orchestra—is the county museum in Asotin. Steep slopes leading up to the rugged Blue Mountains carry such thin plant cover that any grazing beast, cow or deer, must work hard for its dinner.

All the way from Clarkston on the Idaho border to Ilwaco at the mouth of the Columbia River, markers identify the Lewis and Clark Trail Highway. In southeast Washington, displays in Chief Timothy State Park (8 miles west of Clarkston), Lyons Ferry State Park (near Palouse Falls), and

Lewis and Clark Trail State Park (5 miles west of Dayton) tell the explorers' story.

The Lewis and Clark Trail follows U.S. 12, tracing a route along which Lewis and Clark returned, hungry, toward St. Louis in 1806. Their journeys testify to enduring hard times in hard country made of basalt.

The great explorers had come west a year earlier along the Snake River—rough then, tamed now into an agreeable boaters' route between the Tri-Cities on the Columbia and Clarkston (or Lewiston, just across the Idaho line).

From Clarkston-Lewiston, U.S. 195 scrambles up a prodigious canyon wall, 1800 vertical feet, without losing sight of the two towns. Then it scribes long, easy arcs across dry-farmed wheat lands past Pullman and on to Spokane.

Walla Walla

One of Washington's earliest settlements, Walla Walla began near the mission of Dr. Marcus Whitman. The contemporary town is known as the seat of Whitman College. Well-grown deciduous trees shade the quiet streets, a contrast to the sagebrush and evergreen outside town.

The region, incidentally, makes an easy change-of-pace day trip from Pasco-Kennewick-Richland, some 40 miles to the west. U.S. 12 and State 124 form a loop through constantly changing terrain and regularly changing crops. Walla Walla has ample accommodations for overnight stays.

Wineries. On the U.S. 12 approach to town, the community of Lowden is home to three wineries. All are open for tours and tasting, but call first: Waterbrook, (509) 522-1918; L'Ecole, (509) 525-0920; Woodward Canyon, (509) 525-4129.

Whitman Mission. Here in 1836 Dr. Marcus Whitman set up a mission. The following year the Cayuse Indians, victims of a deadly measles epidemic and increased encroachment by settlers, massacred the missionary, his wife Narcissa, and 11 others. Today the mission grounds have a visitor center that amplifies the details of the settlement. A picnic area is set among trees on a green lawn. The mission is 7 miles west of town, just off U.S. 12. It is open daily.

Fort Walla Walla Park. At the southwestern edge of town on the site of a military reservation established in 1858, Fort Walla Walla Park has campsites tucked into cool glens of cottonwood and birch alongside Garrison Creek.

The Fort Walla Walla museum complex includes a reconstruction of a pioneer village. Among the buildings are a one-room schoolhouse and a smithy.

Bluewood Ski Area, 23 miles from Dayton, is within reach of Walla Walla (52 miles), Tri-Cities

(86 miles), and Clarkston (94 miles). Its triple chair and platter pull serve 20 ski runs. The vertical drop is 1,125 feet from a top elevation of 5,670 feet. It also operates a cross-country track. The day lodge has a cafeteria.

The Snake River

Like several reaches of the Columbia, which it joins at the Tri-Cities, the Snake River has ample water in its streambed and virtually none beyond its banks. Sometimes gently sloped, more often in towering walls, the countryside beyond the river seldom offers more than bare basalt to the wondering eye.

Upriver into Idaho from Lewiston and Clarkston is the famed Hells Canyon of the Snake. You can reach the rugged canyon via jet boat from these twin cities.

Heading in the other direction, as the Snake winds along the Idaho border and then into Washington, boaters have the best of it. In the 30 miles between Clarkston and Lower Granite Dam, the Snake burrows along at the bottom of the 2,000-foot-deep, almost vertical-walled canyon it has carved in the several millennia since a great volcanic outpouring buried almost all of eastern Washington under a thick layer of basalt. No road goes near this awesome excavation. Several other scenic stretches, pale only in comparison, can also be seen only from the river.

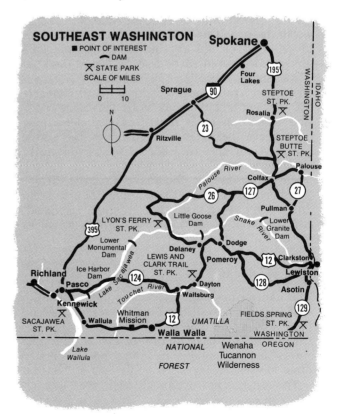

SOUTHEAST WASHINGTON

■ POINT OF INTEREST
⌒ DAM
✗ STATE PARK
SCALE OF MILES
0   10

Dams. For the roadbound in summer, four dams and several parks give regular cooling access to the water at the expense of detours, mostly from U.S. 12. From east to west, the four dams on the Snake are Lower Granite (30 miles downriver from Clarkston), Little Goose (another 30 miles downriver), Lower Monumental (yet another 30 miles downstream, or 60 miles from the confluence with the Columbia at the Tri-Cities), and Ice Harbor (just 10 miles from the Columbia). Each of the four has locks offering free passage to pleasure boats and commercial traffic. All four also have self-guided tours of powerhouses and fish ladders, and—perhaps most welcome—each has a riverside picnic park.

Parks. Just 8 miles west of Clarkston, Chief Timothy State Park offers an interpretive center dealing with local history and geology. The park also has water-related activities.

Boyer Park, downstream from Lower Granite Dam, has both tent and R.V. campsites and food service as well as boat launch, swimming beach, and picnic sites.

Central Ferry State Park, just off State 127 on the north bank of the river, has 60 hookups and a boat launch, a swimming beach, and picnic sites.

State 261 gives access to the settlement of Lyon's Ferry, Lyon's Ferry State Park, and nearby Palouse Falls State Park. Lyon's Ferry and Palouse Falls state parks are administered as a single 1,277-acre unit. Lyon's Ferry has 50 campsites.

In springtime, when snowmelt waters feed the Palouse River, the detour to Palouse Falls is worth the time. Out of nowhere, from what seems to be dry rock, the roaring torrent of the falls plunges 200 feet in hasty descent toward the level of the Snake.

A hiking trail along the canyon wall connects the falls part of the park with the main riverside recreation area. Indian cave shelters now lie beneath the waters backed up by the Lower Granite Dam; they were the reason for the trail's construction.

For parks lower on the Snake, see page 101.

Fishermen work all the dammed pools of the Snake for bass, catfish, shad, salmon, steelhead, and sturgeon. Water-skiers travel miles to get to these ideally calm pools.

Blue Mountains

The name rings true. As visitors approach from east, north, or west, the Blue Mountains rise up hazy, smoky, and blue in the distance.

Up close, the hazy quality of the Blues evaporates. These mountains are craggy basalt. Fir and other forests cover bony ribs only part of the time.

The range is not awesomely high: only a handful of peaks top 6,000 feet. Yet this is isolated, nearly roadless country. Most of the range on Washington's side of the border lies within the Umatilla National Forest. A great part of the forest is set aside as the Wenaha-Tucannon Wilderness, in which 150 miles of trails are the preserve of backpackers and equestrians. (Most of the Blues and most of Umatilla National Forest are across the border in Oregon.)

Hunters come for deer and elk. Fishermen come for rainbow and Dolly Varden trout, especially to the Tucannon River. Hikers come for trails free of rackety motors.

Access is intermittent. From Clarkston, State 129 drifts south to Fields Spring State Park, a 456-acre, 20-campsite gateway to the backcountry. Starting near the park, a dirt road winds up to the edge of the wilderness area. About 25 miles west of Pomeroy, the Tucannon River crosses U.S. 12. At that point a paved road heads into the mountains, in company with the river. Where the paved road ends, the riverside Tucannon Campground (11 tent, 5 R.V. sites) caters to fishermen. It is the largest and most developed of a dozen Forest Service campgrounds in Washington's segment of Umatilla National Forest.

There are ranger stations at Walla Walla, (509) 522-6290, and Pomeroy, (509) 843-1891.

The Palouse

Any longtime sports fan reads "Palouse" and "Washington State University" as synonyms. WSU does pervade the region one way and another, but there is more to it.

Pullman and Washington State University. Pullman is a small town filled with specialty shops and pizza parlors. (Nearby Moscow, Idaho, shares the duties as the regional commercial center.) WSU's campus, on a hill just east of town, dominates the scene. The town and the campus together operate 16 museums; a complete guide is available from the Chamber of Commerce.

Connor Museum specializes in northwestern vertebrates but represents birds and animals of all the Americas. It is closed for remodeling and will reopen in the fall of 1989.

The Museum of Anthropology constantly changes its exhibits, which focus on northwest Indians. The university is notably active in the field, maintaining archaeological digs at several points as well as living contacts. It is open daily except Monday.

Water in an unlikely place
The Palouse River is one of many that have carved courses deep into Eastern Washington's basalt plateau.